Praise for
Applied Insurance Analytics

"Pat Saporito is one of the sharpest minds in the IT business for insurance and financial services. Her deep understanding of the playing field and her devotion to analytics as a key to optimum business processes is unmatched. In particular, Pat really gets it when it comes to the critical importance of the business/IT relationship, and she knows how to apply her wit and wisdom to make all the players around her better."

—Ara Trembly, Founder, The Tech Consultant

"Pat's vast experience, knowledge and insights come to life in this book, a must read for all insurers."

—Deb Smallwood, Founder, Strategy Meets Action

"Finally, Pat has provided a data analytics roadmap for insurance industry decision makers—not just research, but applied research to our industry."

—John A. Cherba, Past President, Society of Insurance Research

"Pat Saporito is that rare individual who understands the business end of insurance and can then match business needs with the supporting technology. She cuts right through the jargon with specific insights about insurance business needs, the data at the heart of our business, and applying analytics for optimal outcomes. Essential reading for anyone who needs to leverage data to drive business results.

"Pat worked closely with me as an advisor to the Institutes' Associate in Information Technology (AIT) program and also with the Insurance Data Management Association (IDMA). Anyone studying analytics or insurance data (such as the AIDM or CIDM from IDMA) will find this to be valuable supplemental reading and a treasured reference."

—Martin J. Frappolli, CPCU, FIDM, Senior Director of
Knowledge Resources, The Institutes (Institute for Chartered Property
Casualty Underwriters and Insurance Institute of America)

"Pat's experience, knowledge, and know-how make her one of the few insurance data professionals who can provide practical and reasonable advice and insight on data uses and needs to carriers and insurance organizations."

—Bill Jenkins, Managing Partner, Agile Insurance Analytics and former CIO,
Penn National Insurance

"As we move into a time with big data and cognitive computing, we are very fortunate as an industry to have thought leadership that brings front and center—as Pat has discussed in her book—topics that we must incorporate and look to as points of reference and most importantly, lessons learned. Great reference materials and perspectives!"

—Cindy Maike, Associate Partner, Insurance, Global Business Services, IBM

"Pat Saporito is acknowledged by all who know her as the consummate industry thought leader. Given her range of experience from the business to IT and analytics, she is a tireless evangelist for communication among all the parties that make our industry tick. I am excited about her using her passion for analytics to empower the business users and their technology partners."

—Beth Grossman, Chief Learning Officer, ACORD

"Pat Saporito is both an insurance industry analytics thought leader and a pragmatist. She uses her extensive industry experience to help insurers understand key use cases and then makes them come to life using actual industry case studies."

—Dennis A. Steckler, Partner, Global Insurance Solutions, Return on Intelligence, Inc.

"I have had the pleasure to work with Pat on a number of occasions to talk with clients about the business value of analytics. Pat knows this better than anyone I know. In her book, she connects the dots between business challenges and analytics capabilities in the insurance industry and provides a roadmap on how to optimize analytics in practice."

—Dwight McNeill, Professor and Author of
*A Framework for Applying Analytics in Healthcare:
What Can Be Learned from the Best Practices in
Retail, Banking, Politics, and Sports.*

"Pat provides an in-depth analysis and guideline to the competitive advantage weapon for the Insurance industry winners of the future. The difference between winners and losers will be analytics—Pat provides an in-depth guide for successful adoption."

—Piyush Singh, CPCU, SVP and CIO, Great American Insurance Co.

APPLIED INSURANCE ANALYTICS

APPLIED INSURANCE ANALYTICS

A FRAMEWORK FOR DRIVING MORE VALUE FROM DATA ASSETS, TECHNOLOGIES, AND TOOLS

Patricia L. Saporito

Associate Publisher: Amy Neidlinger
Executive Editor: Jeanne Glasser Levine
Operations Specialist: Jodi Kemper
Cover Designer: Alan Clements
Managing Editor: Kristy Hart
Project Editor: Elaine Wiley
Copy Editor: Apostrophe Editing Services
Proofreader: The Wordsmithery LLC
Indexer: Lisa Stumpf
Senior Compositor: Gloria Schurick
Manufacturing Buyer: Dan Uhrig

For information about buying this title in bulk quantities, or for special sales opportunities (which may include electronic versions; custom cover designs; and content particular to your business, training goals, marketing focus, or branding interests), please contact our corporate sales department at corpsales@pearsoned.com or (800) 382-3419.

For government sales inquiries, please contact governmentsales@pearsoned.com.

For questions about sales outside the U.S., please contact international@pearsoned.com.

Company and product names mentioned herein are the trademarks or registered trademarks of their respective owners.

Printed in the United States of America

2   16

ISBN-10: 0-13-376036-7
ISBN-13: 978-0-13-376036-1

Pearson Education LTD.
Pearson Education Australia PTY, Limited.
Pearson Education Singapore, Pte. Ltd.
Pearson Education Asia, Ltd.
Pearson Education Canada, Ltd.
Pearson Educación de Mexico, S.A. de C.V.
Pearson Education—Japan
Pearson Education Malaysia, Pte. Ltd.

Library of Congress Control Number: 2014937548

Contents

About the Author

Pat Saporito is a senior director for SAP's Global Center of Excellence for BI and Analytics. She is SAP's thought leader for analytics in the insurance industry. In her role she provides thought leadership and guidance to help customers leverage their data and technology investments. In addition to insurance she has worked with many other industries including airlines, banking, consumer products, healthcare, manufacturing, mining, oil and gas, and utilities.

Pat is a faculty member of the International Institute for Analytics (IIA), co-founded by Tom Davenport, and is a frequent speaker at industry and analytics events on the topics of data warehousing, analytics, and BI Strategy. Pat authored the chapter on business value in the recently published IIA book, *Analytics in Healthcare and the Life Sciences*.

Pat has been a columnist for *Best's Review* magazine's Technology Insights column for the past 10 years. She has blogged in various social media outlets. Pat has served in numerous industry roles. She is past president of the Society of Insurance Research, past chair of the Society of Chartered Property and Casualty Underwriters (CPCU) Information Technology Section, has been a director of Insurance Data Management Association, and has been an education committee member of Insurance Accounting & Systems Association (IASA). She is also past president of APIW, an organization of executive insurance women.

Pat holds the Society of CPCU professional designation and has been awarded a Fellow of Insurance Data Management by the Insurance Data Management Association (IDMA) in recognition of her advocacy of and contributions to the field of data management and analytics.

Twitter: @PatSaporito

LinkedIn: www.linkedin/in/patriciasaporito

Preface

I have spent more than 20 years working with business users and IT staff using information and technology and have seen both raving successes and raging failures. I have been involved in building both transactional systems as well as analytic applications. Analytics is a field that I am passionate about because I have seen first-hand the impacts that effective analytics can have on the insurance industry and more importantly on our customers. I wrote this book to share my experiences and provide an understanding of analytic capabilities and key considerations in using analytics and building analytic applications for the insurance industry.

I have been a business analyst, a systems owner, a technology consultant, and a management consultant. Failures nearly always result from a lack of communication between business and IT due to differences in expectations and experience. I have seen brilliantly designed data warehouses that were never used by the business. In other words, if you build it they will not come unless it actually meets their needs.

The primary audience for this book is business users; I have kept technical jargon to a minimum and have used common terms that business people will most likely encounter in working with their IT partners. I have purposely omitted references to many important technological functions performed in administration, operations, and architecture, which fall under the chief information officer (CIO) or chief technology officer (CTO). If you are a technical person, I recommend that you read this book from the perspective of the business user; this view can help you improve your alignment and better understand the business needs, especially in the use cases and case studies in Chapter 10, "Use Cases and Case Studies." You should also find the section on business discovery useful in Chapter 11, "Future of Insurance Analytics," because it is critical to extracting these needs.

I began my insurance career as a claims adjuster where I developed interviewing skills that have served me well as both a business analyst and management consultant, and more relevantly in analytics for business discovery and value analysis. As I advanced in my claims career,

I assumed responsibility for field operations and also became the owner of record for the claims administration systems. I moved into IT where I became a business analyst and then a business systems architect and later into a research and development role evaluating technologies for business innovation and new product development. I had my own market research and information management consulting business for 6 years. I have been a technology analyst; I led an insurance industry research service. I then joined the vendor community where I ran a team of industry consultants for the insurance, healthcare, and pharmaceutical industries for a data warehousing vendor and conducted many data warehousing and analytic business discoveries. At my current employer, I have held multiple roles, including analytic insurance solutions management and management consulting. I have worked not only with insurance and healthcare, but also with many other industries including airlines, banking, consumer products, manufacturing, and utilities. In my role in an Analytics Center of Excellence I meet with customers to help them evaluate and advance their analytics maturity using leading practices. I have tried to incorporate experiences and lessons that I have learned along the way into this book.

I have benefited from being mentored and befriended during my career by too many people to name, but I would like to recognize the following and offer apologies to any I have mindlessly omitted: Jim Anastasio, Sandra Ballew, Michael Bernaski, Russ Bingham, Peter Bogdon, Steve Boley, Lamont Boyd, Bill Burns, Art Cadorine, Fran Chemaly, Jack Cherba, Steve Collesano, Chris Christy, Reilly Cobb, Judy DeMouth, Sue Koral, Diana Lee, Ken Levey, Lee McDonald, Cindy Maike, David Moorhead, Anthony O'Donnell, Joe Peloso, Roland Perkins, Peri Pieroni, Shannon Platz, Rick Porter, Barry Rabkin, Bill Raichle, Imran Siddiqi, Piyush Singh, Deb Smallwood, Pat Speer, Jay Spence, Maureen Strazdon, Dale Strobel, Ara Tremblay, David Van den Eynde, and Ray Zolonowski. Thank you all for your knowledge, support, and friendship.

I'd also like to thank numerous people who reviewed and provided input for this book including Christian Blumhoff, Louis Bode, Ken Demma, Bill Jenkins, Shane McCullough, Jeri Ostling, Greta Roberts, Dennis Steckler, Nate Root, and Tracy Spadola.

I'd like to extend a special thanks to Dwight McNeill for encouraging me to write this book and introducing me to my editor, Jeanne Levine, at Pearson.

I hope in some small way this book provides payback and inspiration to others.

1

Analytics in Insurance Overview

Insurance is an industry that runs on data. Regardless of the industry segment—Property and Casualty, Life, or Health—insurers provide a service or financial product versus a physical product to policyholders, and most often a promise to pay to or to indemnify on behalf of a policyholder or to invest on behalf of. From the initial marketing and customer insurance shopping and buying experience, through to a claim payment or investment payout, the entire *insurance value chain,* the end-to-end link business processes, are data driven. Data is literally the life blood of the insurance industry and analytics drive overall industry business performance through increased revenue or decreased expenses. It relies on data and analysis to improve financial performance and services to shareholders and policyholders.

Analytics is the discovery and communication of meaningful patterns in data. *Business intelligence (BI)* strictly speaking is a subset of analytics. BI is generally understood to be more narrowly focused on reporting and data visualization technologies such as dashboards. Another area of analytics is *predictive analytics*, which includes data mining, text mining, and predictive modeling. *Advanced visualization* is yet another area of analytics which includes maps, three-dimensional graphics and more sophisticated visual representations beyond tables and simple graphics such as those found in Microsoft Excel. BI and analytics are used interchangeably through this book from a practical perspective.

Analytics improve business processes, decision making, and overall business performance and profitability through insights gleaned and actions taken based on these insights. Analytics rely on the simultaneous application of statistics, computer programming, and operations research to quantify performance. Analytics often use data visualization to communicate insights.

The overall analytics process takes raw data from multiple operational systems, transforms that data so that it is "normalized," (or in the same format regardless of its source), often augments it with external or third-party data, and turns it into information. It then enables analysis and produces insights or observations from the information and, lastly, guides decisions or actions based on the insights made.

Operational Versus Traditional Analytics

Analytics take two major forms: operational analysis and traditional analysis. *Operational analytics*, often referred to as *embedded analytics*, are embedded or built right into the business processes or application systems such as marketing, underwriting, claims adjusting, and so on. Operational analytics are more real time because immediate access to the data brings higher value for certain functions before an action is taken, for example, claim fraud detected during a first notice of loss reporting. It is more effective to identify and prevent paying a fraudulent claim than to pursue the payment recovery.

Traditional analytics such as loss development trend analysis or emerging loss exposure analysis occur after the processing transactions take place and are based on more aggregated analysis. Analytics in both these areas are increasingly using *predictive analytics* to go beyond understanding historical trends about what happened and why, by using leading indicators and correlation metrics to forecast what will happen and even to optimize future business performance

External Data

It's hard to imagine the industry running without analytics as analytics have been so hard-coded into the industry DNA in marketing, underwriting, pricing, and claims with a wealth of data available at the micro or tactical operational level. Yet at the macro or strategic level, when deciding on new products to offer or markets to enter, insurers have limited and sometimes not any internal data. In these cases, insurers can turn to *external data* from third parties such as state insurance department filings, industry composite databases from rating agencies, or public records for information needed to develop new market offerings. Insurers can also use *psychographic data* (psychological or behavioral data plus demographic) as proxies for target marketing and even underwriting characteristics, for example, income, occupation, and so on. Even when insurers have data, they often use external data to augment and enrich their internal data.

Table 1-1 shows common business functions where third-party data is used, how it is used (use case), and the type of data used.

Table 1-1 External Data Sources

Function	Use Case	Third-Party Data Type/Source
Marketing	Marketing Campaigns	Psychographic
Product Management	New Product Development, Pricing	State Insurance Rate Filings
Claims	Subrogation Recoveries	Warranty Data, Product Recalls
Underwriting	Risk Profile Enhancement, UW Risk Assessment	Motor Vehicle Records (MVRs) Credit Reports
Sales	Lead Generation	College Alumni Records
Medical Management	Health and Wellness Management	Prescription

The following descriptions provide more detail on the above Use Cases:

- Marketing has used psychographic data to augment existing customer data or as proxies for customer data in target marketing. Profiling characteristics of existing customers, it looks for similar traits in prospects.

- Product managers often review competitor rate filings to compare products and product pricing, as well as target markets.

- Claims recovery analysts have used warranty data and product recall data to augment claims and underwriting data for claims involving defective products. Two examples are sport utility vehicle rollovers involving faulty tires and kitchen fires that originated in dishwashers or stoves.

- Underwriting has used credit scores as part of its underwriting risk models, where allowable.

- Sales management and producers have used various sources such as college alumni records for lead generation.

- Medical managers are using prescription data and even retail data from drug stores to profile members as part of their wellness and disease management programs.

Insurance Industry Data Flow

To understand and apply analytics effectively, it is essential to understand how data is created and processed, and how it flows throughout the organization. Figure 1-1 traces data from data originators on the left, across the business processes with key metrics by process, how it flows to the accounting systems and general ledger, and ultimately to statistical reporting. Although the example is for Property and Casualty, the flows are similar for Life and Health industry segments.

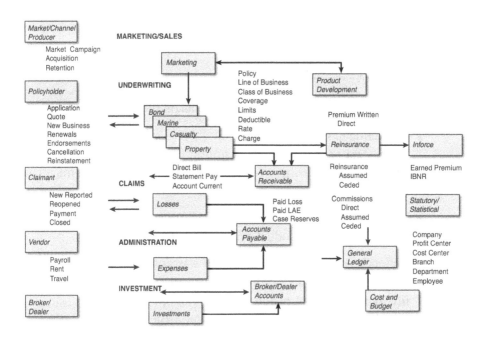

Figure 1-1 Property and Casualty Industry Data Flow

Analytic Maturity

Analytic maturity, or the increasing sophistication in the use of analytics, is based on a number of factors. Following are the four key factors:

- **People:** How analytically sophisticated the employee area is (and how data driven the organizational culture is)

- **Process:** How mature the analytic processes within an organization are

- **Technology:** What tools have been selected, deployed, and made available to employees

- **Data:** How well data is managed, governed, and made available within the organization

Figure 1-2 shows different analytic maturity levels.

Reactive ———————————————————————→ Proactive

	Analytics Laggards	Analytics Aspirers	Analytics Novices	Analytic Practitioners	Analytic Savants
People	• Gut Based Decisioning	• Analytic Awareness • Use Analytics to validate Gut	• Tactical Decisioning	• Support Strategic Decisions	• Drive Strategy • Embedded in DNA • Chief Analytics Officer
Process	• None	• Ask others for analytic reports	• Create own reports • Analysis vs. Reporting	• BICC • Business participates as Business Analyst, Data Steward	• Analytic Mentors • Mature BICC • Analytic Communities of Practice
Technology	• Excel	• Standard Rtpg • Limited Ad Hoc Rptg	• Ad Hoc Rptg • Dashboards	• Visualization • Data Exploration	• Predictive • Text Mining • Sentiment Analysis
Data	• Data Silos • Poor Data Quality	• Spreadmarts • Data Quality Awareness	• Data Marts • Data Dictionary	• Integrated Data Views • Data Governance	• Embedded Analytics • Data as strategic corporate asset

Figure 1-2 Analytics Continuum Matrix

Key Insurance Analytics

Key analytic application areas within insurance are

- Marketing analytics used for customer segmentation, cross-sell and upsell, marketing campaign management;
- Product management analytics used for product management and product profitability;
- Underwriting analytics used for risk assessment and pricing;
- Claims analytics used for claim valuation, reserving, settlement and recoveries, and fraud detection;
- Enterprise risk analytics for solvency and capital allocation;
- Sales analytics for channel and producer management, and incentive compensation management;
- Finance management for planning, budgeting and forecasting, and profitability analysis.

These areas will be explored in depth with use cases and example case studies in Chapter 10, "Use Cases and Case Studies." Figure 1-3 shows an overview of commonly used analytics by business process.

Figure 1-3 Key Insurance Processes and Analytics

Analytics Users and Usability

Literally every function in the industry uses analytics: actuaries, underwriters, claims professionals, loss control specialists, marketing professionals, finance analysts, customer service representatives, agents and brokers, and regulators. Everyone in the insurance value chain needs and uses some form of analytics.

However, within these functional areas, different roles have different analytic needs. Executive management, such as CEOs, and board and senior management want key metrics in an easily consumable and highly visual format: dashboards or score cards, and increasingly on mobile devices such as tablets or mobile phones. Middle management wants key operational dashboards with more navigation including drill to detail and often standard or ad hoc reports and desktop, as well as mobile access. Analysts want yet even more detail plus the ability to manipulate data, create additional metrics, and even create their own reports/analytic views. Tools are reviewed further in Chapter 7, "Analytics Tools."

Challenges

Yet as much as analytics are needed, analytic adoption often falls short because insurance stakeholders face a myriad of challenges using analytics.

First and foremost, insurance stakeholders often lack *data access* to complete, trusted, and understandable data. Insurers should strive not just for quality, but for trusted data that is well documented, that can be used for its intended purpose, and where any "nuances" in the data are understood. Data can also be augmented; for example, structured data can be augmented with unstructured data such as text data from customer surveys or customer sentiment data from social media. A solid *data governance* process can ensure the documentation of existing data and define new data needed. Often the best "home" for data governance in an insurance company is in actuarial or finance departments because both are responsible for internal and external reporting and have a high interest in data quality and integrity. Further, these areas often use data from across multiple business domains and are familiar with the challenges in integrating data.

A second hurdle is a lack of or limitation in **analytic skills**, which inhibits effective use of analytics. One cause is cultural, often due to a lack of awareness or perhaps lethargy. All too often we rely on gut instinct for decisions. We mistake reporting for analysis. Data exploration and data visualization, enabled by user-friendly tools, are helping enterprise employees improve their analysis and their analytic insights. In addition, organizations are hiring new employees with analytic skills and developing the skills of existing employees. Those organizations who invest in ongoing analytic skill development will see higher analytic adoption and increased employee satisfaction and retention.

Yet a third barrier is the **analytic tools** themselves. It's important to select and use the right tool for the right analysis and the right user. At one extreme, executives want to use highly visual, summarized analytics through dashboards and mobile devices. At the other end, analysts are looking for robust tools that allow them to manipulate and merge or augment data, create new calculations, and perform complex analysis. "Data scientists," who include marketing analysts, finance analysts, and actuarial analysts, want even more robust predictive and statistical capabilities. Many companies have formed **BI Competency Centers or Centers of Excellence** to provide training, encourage end user analytic tool adoption, and engage business users in the evaluation and selection of new tools as well as to define and execute an overall BI strategy and to provide overall governance.

Technologies continue to evolve. Enterprise information management tools allow companies to better access and integrate data; to scrub it, to understand its source, and to understand the impact on existing analytics if it is added to or changed. In memory, databases provide increased performance and speed for cranking through ever more granular data for actuarial pricing and reserving analysis. Geographic Positioning

Systems (GPS) and geomapping technologies enable organizations to augment risk and loss data to better understand underwriting risk and loss patterns. Visualization tools enable users to make more sense of market and customer data. Organizations have access to machine-generated data through devices in automobile insurance; similarly, they can integrate data from medical devices providing biofeedback for health insurance and wellness monitoring and intervention. User interfaces go beyond the desktop or laptop, to mobile not just for field employees like agents, loss inspection, and claims professionals but for all employees—data anywhere, anytime, on any device making data security critical as data and analytics access become ubiquitous.

Insurance Analytics Evolution

Insurers increase their analytic maturity as they improve their data management and metric sophistication. As they increase data granularity and data quality and integrate it across more than one functional area or business domain, they enable more sophisticated analytics. Similarly, as they measure not only historical key performance indicators but also the leading indicators (or driving analytics), they also enable more predictive analytics within and across functional areas.

Figure 1-4 reviews the maturity evolution for a subset of insurance processes: marketing, product development, pricing, underwriting, and claims. The overall industry analytic maturity is indicated with the dots. A useful exercise is for individual organizations to assess their maturity, compare it to where they aspire to be, and to identity the hurdles that keep them from reaching their desired state. Following this self-assessment, they can define plans to address areas of needed improvement to reach their next level of maturity and use analytics for strategic competitive advantage.

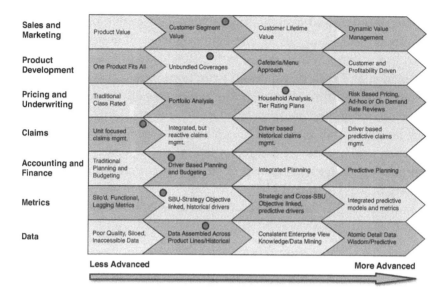

Figure 1-4 Insurance Analytics Evolution

Summary

Learning Objectives

Test your basic knowledge of the main points in this chapter by answering the following questions:

- Name major insurance business processes and key analytics used by these processes.

- Review how data originates and flows across and outside the organization.

- Apply the Insurance Analytics Evolution Framework to measure maturity.

Discussion Questions

Further check your application of key concepts by reviewing the following discussion questions:

- Describe how analytics are used in marketing, sales, underwriting, claims, and finance.

- Identify and explain three external data sources and what analytics areas they can be used in.

- Discuss the three challenges in effectively using analytics and how they can be overcome.

Key Terms

Analytic maturity refers to the increasing sophistication in the use of analytics and involves four key dimensions of analytic users, analytic processes, analytic technologies, and data.

Business Intelligence Competency Center (or Center of Excellence) is a corporate function that defines and executes a strategic business intelligence program through BI Governance committees.

Data governance is a corporate process that ensures data quality and data understandability. It involves a Data Governance council and includes data stewards from various business areas who participate in this process.

Operational analytics are analytics used within a transactional system such as claims management; these would include a list of new claims created, a list of claims open more than 30 days, and so on.

Predictive analytics are analytics that use historical data to forecast future results. These include data mining, text mining, predictive models, and so on.

Additional Resources/Reading

"The Data-Driven Organization." Marcia W. Blenko, Michael C. Mankins, Paul Rogers. *Harvard Business Review.* June 2010.

2

Analytics Strategy and Execution Framework

D ata is a key asset for insurers, but to maximize the business value of this asset, insurers need a business-driven enterprise approach to *analytics*: an enterprise analytic strategy. Effective IT strategies are designed, built, and executed with a "think big, but start small" approach that defines a strategic roadmap and delivers results tactically proving value project by project within the overarching strategy.

IT organizations often embark on an enterprise analytics effort to build the "all singing, all dancing" enterprise *data warehouse*. They interview business users about their needs and run off to design a data model to organize the data and start loading data into a data warehouse. But the business is looking for the analytics—now. By the time IT delivers the analytics, business priorities have likely changed such that the analytics are no longer relevant or the business area has found another way to obtain the analytics with whatever tools it could find. The business areas build *data marts* causing data silos and conflicting reports that require much of their time reconciling data versus using the analytics. Sound awful and awfully familiar? To avoid this, IT needs to engage the business early and continuously to define and implement the strategy with discrete deliverables, ensuring data confidence and communicating the results and value of the results delivered. IT needs a *BI strategy* and can build one with the business using a BI Strategy Framework.

BI Strategy Framework

A Business Intelligence (or Analytic) Strategy Framework encompasses five major areas:

- **Objectives and scope:** The purpose and objective of your strategy—its current state and history; and your analytic objectives and scope (what's included and, as important, what's not).

- **Business needs:** A summary of your BI needs from the business perspective by business functional area (marketing, sales, underwriting, claims, finance, customer service, and so on) and the best tools to fulfill them (reporting, geographic information systems, data mining, text mining, self-service, mobile, dashboards, and so on); your vision or to-be state; and your priorities and alignment (agreement within the organization as to the prioritization of fulfilling the business needs).

NOTE:

The latter should be done within the context of the overall corporate and individual business unit business strategy; the definition, prioritization and alignment is most often achieved through conducting a business discovery, a facilitated interview process to extract the business needs, anticipated business value, strategic and tactical alignment, and data leverage across business units.

- **Value:** The business value of analytics expressed quantitatively; the expected benefits, including future state Key Performance Indicators (KPIs) for adoption, effectiveness, and efficiency goals, and so on; business case formats both for the original strategy and for ongoing initiatives/projects; post-implementation measurement; and a value-based management approach that includes the processes and methodologies in business case and post implementation review.

- **Information structure and technology:** Your information categories/domain definitions, (customer/member, agent, policy, claims, financial, and so on); architecture and standards; and BI tools and analytic applications.

- **Organization and governance:** Your governance structure (including steering and working committees), program management, BI roadmap and milestones, measurement approach and methodology for BI adoption and organization value to ensure funding, education and training (including defining programs and measuring how effective they are), and ongoing support. Organizational change and user adoption are critical components in this area as well to ensure user adoption and a decision-driven organization.

Figure 2-1 provides an overview of the five key elements in a strategic business intelligence and analytics program.

Figure 2-1 BI Strategy Framework

Many organizations mistake an architecture diagram for a BI strategy. The architecture is important, but it is only one element of the overall strategy. Following are other tell-tale signs that an organization does not have a formalized strategy:

- **IT asks business areas what reports they need.** This is a good start, but analytics are more than just reports; a strategy needs to also include analytics and data, not just reporting.

- **The first step in the analytics strategy is building a data warehouse.** IT needs to make sure it understands the business needs before it embarks on building the warehouse. This is critical to prioritizing the roadmap to user participation and funding.

- **Neither BI team nor business team members can articulate the BI strategy.** This is usually because it has not been defined, documented, or communicated. Both areas need to understand the strategy to work together effectively.

- **There are no metrics defined to measure progress.** This means you cannot objectively measure your progress, nor report on it. Your progress must be transparent and accessible so that you can recognize success and identify and address issues.

Business Intelligence Competency Center

Leading practice is to execute a BI strategy through a *BI Competency Center (BICC)* or *BI Center of Excellence (COE),* whose mission is to define and update the strategy and ensure its governance. The BICC is the link between IT developers and the business.

An effective BI strategy also needs executive sponsorship and *governance* in the form of various committees to set priorities, commit funding, and resolve inevitable issues and conflicts. The BICC role is primarily governance. It works side by side with the BI development team that maintains the infrastructure and data and delivers BI projects. The BICC may reside in IT and report to the CIO, or it may reside in a business area and report to a senior business officer such as the chief administrative officer (CAO) or chief strategy officer (CSO) or to a new role, the chief analytics officer (CAO).

Further detail on the BICC role, governance structures, program management, development of BI roadmap and milestones, BI measurement, education and training, and end user support are addressed in Chapter 8, "Organization and Implementation."

Executive Sponsorship and Key Roles

Executive sponsorship and alignment are keys to an effective BI strategy definition, execution, and ongoing funding. The senior management team should be interviewed and updated annually on the organization's strategy and current status. Figures 2-2, 2-3, and 2-4 show examples of insurance industry organization charts for property and casualty, life, and health insurers.

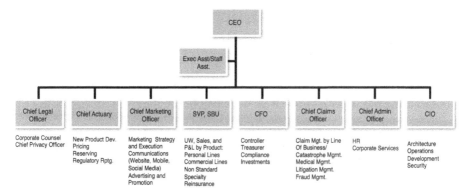

Figure 2-2 Example Insurance Organization Chart—Property and Casualty

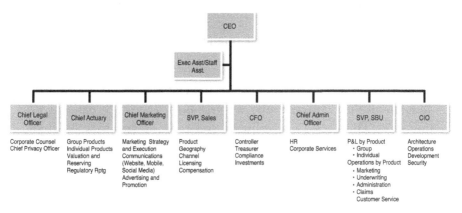

Figure 2-3 Example Insurance Organization Chart—Life

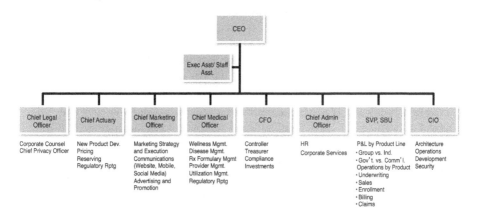

Figure 2-4 Example Insurance Organization Chart—Health

Emerging C-Level Analytics Roles

In addition to the senior management team, there are several key BI strategy-related roles that are emerging across industries.

- *Chief analytics officer* (CAO) is an emerging senior-level management position that is responsible for defining an organization's analytics strategy from a business perspective.

- *Chief data officer (CDO)* is a similar role that focused on the data management versus the analytics; it often resides in IT. In some organizations the chief analytics officer may also hold the CDO role.

- *Chief science officer (CSO)* is a third role that is also surfacing. This role is focused on the use of *advanced analytics* and statistics for predictive modeling to drive future business performance.

Insurance and other financial services industry sectors have been early adopters of the CAO and related roles, as they are such data-driven industries. However, these roles are still evolving and have different titles, scope, and levels of authority from organization to organization. Table 2-1 describes these new roles.

Table 2-1 Emerging C-Level Analytics Roles

Role	Definition
Chief analytics officer (CAO)	Responsible for the analytic strategy of an organization. Is responsible for both the analytic strategy and application of analytics in the business. Often reports to the CEO. Works with the CIO, CDO, and CSO. Has strong management consulting experience; has often held CSO role.
Chief data officer (CDO)	Responsible for enterprise-wide governance and utilization of information as a corporate asset. Works with CAO, CIO, CTO, and Chief Data (Security) Officer. Often chairs or is an executive member of the Data Governance Committee. Role may reside in business or in IT. May be merged with CAO.

Role	Definition
Chief science officer (CSO)	Responsible for advanced analytics such as predictive modeling, data mining, and predictive. May be a business or an IT role. Works closely with CAO and CIO. Role may be merged with CAO. Strong statistics, economics, and/or econometrics background.

Before these new roles appeared, in insurance the chief actuarial officer (CAO) or chief financial officer (CFO) often effectively held the role of chief data officer (CDO) and chaired data governance committees, as these two roles have the responsibility for external regulatory reporting to the SEC, state insurance departments, and rating agencies and have a key vested interest in data accuracy. Poor data quality can result in not only rework for filings, but also a loss of credibility with regulators, potential compliance fines, and even loss of reputation and market value.

It remains to be seen if chief actuaries or CFOs will assume the broader role of chief analytics officer (CAO) or if they will assume the responsibilities for chief data officer (CDO) within their current roles.

Summary

Learning Objectives

Test your basic knowledge of the main points in this chapter by answering the following questions:

- Understand the need for a Business Intelligence strategy and the parts of a BI strategy framework.

- Comprehend the role of a BI Competency Center (or Center of Excellence) in BI strategy definition and execution.

- Review C-Level roles that need to be engaged in providing executive leadership for a BI strategy.

Discussion Questions

Further check your application of key concepts by reviewing the following discussion questions:

- Name the five key elements of a BI strategy and describe key elements that they include.

- Describe the BICC role as it relates to BI governance.

- Compare and contrast the roles of the chief analytics officer (CAO), chief data officer (CDO), and chief data scientist.

Key Terms

Advanced Analytics includes applications and technologies that leverage historical, current, and predictive data to help an organization analyze and make decisions to optimize business performance. They include data mining, predictive modeling, "what if" simulations (sensitivity analysis), statistics, opinion mining, and text mining. These analytics are used to identify meaningful patterns and correlations in data sets to predict future events and potential outcomes.

Analytics incudes the data, tools, and applications that support corporate strategic plans and business performance; they provide the ability to gather, store, access, and analyze corporate data for decision making. Analytics is increasingly being used interchangeably with *Business Intelligence*, which initially focused on reporting but has expanded into broader areas such as data exploration and visualization. *Advanced analytics* is often used to describe predictive analytics.

BI Competency Center (BICC) or BI Center of Excellence (COE) is an organization with a mission to define and update the BI strategy and ensure its governance. The BICC is the link between BI developers and the business.

BI governance is the corporate process that provides oversight and includes various committees to set priorities, commit funding, and resolve inevitable issues and conflicts. BI governance is overseen by the BICC.

BI strategy refers to a strategic, programmatic approach to business intelligence and analytics as opposed to a fragmented or tactical perspective.

Data marts are analytic data stores that are limited to a functional or departmental focus; they are usually used for reporting to support specific functional analytics, for example, data mining. They are often extracted as a subset of a data warehouse.

Data warehouses are enterprise data stores used for analytic analysis and decisioning. They involve physical or logical extraction of data from transactional processing systems, which is transformed into a "rationalized," or integrated view, of the data from multiple sources, internal and external.

Additional Resources/Reading

"Business Intelligence in Plain Language: A practical guide to Data Mining and Business Analytics." Jeremy Kolb. Applied Data Labs, Inc. 2012.

The BI Competency Center – 2012 Study. Cap Gemini. 2012.

3

Defining, Prioritizing, and Aligning Needs

Defining, prioritizing, and aligning business needs are always a challenge. Every business area believes that its own analytic needs are the most important and gets frustrated when these needs are not met or not met on as timely a basis as they want. The initial challenge is to define business needs effectively so that IT can understand them, prioritize them in light of various area needs, and determine what data and capabilities can be leveraged across business areas. They are one of the key five elements of a BI strategy, as shown in Figure 3-1.

Figure 3-1 BI Strategy Framework—Business Needs

Business needs are most frequently documented by business analysts who usually sit in a business area but can also reside in IT. Often business analysts in IT are former business users. Using common requirements templates helps ensure consistent and effective requirements and shortens the time required to define them. Effective templates provide enough information for IT to understand the needs but are not so onerous that business users are discouraged from completing them.

These should be limited to no more than 10 questions and encompass these broad categories:

- **Data:** Current versus future access, quality, completeness, and currentness; capabilities: extraction, integration, and so on

- **Metrics:** Existence and use of metrics frameworks defined including KPIs, metrics, leading indicators and correlations

- **Analysis:** Current versus future needs and capabilities, including reporting, dashboards, exploration, and visualization

- **Tools:** Existing versus needed tools and capabilities, including mobile, self-service, and so on

- **Training and skills:** Existing versus future skills; training platforms and training available; mentoring capabilities; and communities of practice

- **Strategy:** Alignment between business and IT strategies

Business Needs Definition Approaches

One of the most frequently used approaches to define business requirements is a facilitated *business discovery* interview. In this approach, business analysts meet with business users and interview them; they ask users to describe their business needs. Often the business area will be asked to describe its top two to three key business initiatives for the next 12 to 18 months and what analytic capabilities will be needed to support these initiatives (see Table 3-1). In addition, business users are often asked about any gaps or issues in their current analytics. If executives are included in this process, the executive interview is often conducted followed up by a small group interview, usually limited to four to six individuals. The interviews are organized by business function, for example, underwriting, claims, finance, and so on.

Table 3-1   Business Discovery Interview Guide Excerpt—Underwriting

Need/Issue	Benefit	Measurable Value
UNDERWRITING RISK GRANULARITY: Lack granularity of risk data and ability to link across underwriting, marketing, and sales distribution for an integrated underwriting, marketing, and sales strategy. We need access to this information for integrated, effective market positioning.	We will be able to better identify, classify, and price our risks. We will present clear communication of our market appetite and market positioning, improve producer satisfaction, and improve underwriter effectiveness and efficiency from an integrated underwriting, marketing, and distribution strategy.	Increased growth: number of policies × average written premium per policy × time period measured
ABILITY TO TRACK, ASSESS, AND/OR MANAGE COVERAGE GAPS AND LIMITATIONS: Often we don't see trends in coverage gaps or limitations early enough or at all, resulting in producers sending business to competitors or insureds non-renewing their policies after an uncovered or partially covered claim.	Understanding gaps and limitation would provide opportunities for additional coverages and products, as well as help increase our customer retention and producer satisfaction.	Premium and policy growth: total written premium change and policies in force

Need/Issue	Benefit	Measurable Value
VIEWS INTO ENTERPRISE-WIDE DATA AND STRATEGIC PERSPECTIVES INTO CUSTOMER, SALES, POLICY ADMINISTRATION, AND CLAIM PERFORMANCE INDICATORS: When high quality data is not consistently shared across the enterprise, various issues and gaps arise in our ability to analyze our underwriting performance. Various areas may have different or redundant data that can lead to incorrect and/or unnecessary underwriting related actions and efforts.	Data will be collected, managed, and maintained across the enterprise in a consistent manner to address both the broad and narrow needs of the organization that data silos and local data ownership cannot. Increased data governance at the organizational level will help enable standardization of metrics, consistent use for underwriting performance measurement, and reduce staff time in data reconciliation from differing metrics from various areas.	Improved enterprise performance management capabilities; Improved employee effectiveness and efficiencies; More time for analysis versus reconciling data

Another business requirements definition approach used is an *Analytics Actionability Framework*. This is another facilitated approach; in this one, a business user is asked by IT to do the following:

- Define its top two to three key business objectives

- Define the business questions that the business user needs to answer to ensure that it can meet the objective

- Identify what actions it could take if it had the answer to the business questions

- Define the Key Performance Indicators (KPIs) or metrics the user would use to measure improvement

This approach can further be extended to define the data sources needed and data availability for each of these business objectives.

Table 3-2 shows the underwriting with three key objectives: 1) accurate risk classification, rating, and pricing; 2) agent and customer satisfaction and retention; and 3) associate productivity and retention.

Table 3-2 Analytics Actionability Matrix—Underwriting

Objective	Business Questions/ Analysis	Actions	Measureable Results/KPIs
Appropriate Risk Classification, Assessment, and Pricing	■ What risk segment/classification does this class of risks fall into? ■ What are the exposures for this risk/risk class? What is the loss history for this risk/risk class? For this insured/group of insureds? ■ Does this risk/risk class fall within our current underwriting guidelines? If not, can the exposure/coverage/price be modified to make it acceptable? ■ What is the proper price for this risk/risk class? ■ How do we compare to competitors? (price, product, etc.)	■ Plan strategies on growth and profitability targets ■ Align products to spread risk and ensure sufficient premium for exposure ■ Make pricing/terms and condition adjustments based on individual exposure and loss experience	■ Meet target segment and product goals (written premium, PIFs, and profitability) ■ Improved risk portfolio profitability (loss ratio, net underwriting profit) ■ Updated underwriting guidelines
Agent and Customer Satisfaction and Retention	■ What are our new business trends? (new applications/submissions, quotes, policies issued) ■ What are our renewals trends? (renewals, cancellations, non-renewals) ■ What is our customer and agent satisfaction with our products, pricing and service? What are their retention rates?	■ ID and analyze negative new business trends and take action ■ ID and analyze negative renewal trends and take action ■ ID and analyze negative satisfaction trends and take action	■ Meet new business and renewal goals ■ Improved customer and agent satisfaction ■ Improved customer and agent retention

Objective	Business Questions/ Analysis	Actions	Measureable Results/KPIs
Associate Productivity and Retention	■ What is our staff turnover rate? ■ What is the employee satisfaction level? ■ What is the impact to customer and/or agent service?	■ Determine cause for unacceptable turnover rate and take appropriate action ■ Determine reason for poor employee satisfaction and take appropriate action ■ Improve recruitment or training processes	■ Reduced turnover rate ■ Improved employee satisfaction ■ Improved customer and agent service ■ Improved customer and agent satisfaction ■ Improved customer and agent retention

Yet a third approach to define requirements is *Use Cases*. Use Cases can be used for other purposes as well, such as success stories. Use Cases involve an objective or goal, an actor (or actors), and scenarios. Each scenario includes a goal, a primary actor, defined conditions for the scenario, and a scenario result.

Use Cases are usually in narrative form; the narrative may be combined with graphics or flow charts to show multiple actors. They may include extensions or conditions that affect a scenario and variations in the scenario. Following is a narrative Use Case example for Underwriting.

UNDERWRITING USE CASE EXAMPLE

Business Objective: Underwriting Review—New Business—Standard Auto

Primary Actor: Underwriter

Goal: Classify, Assess, and Price New Business Application

Condition: Normal, no exceptional risk conditions

Outcome: Policy Quote and Issue

1. The agent completes the policy application and submits it to the underwriter.

2. The underwriter reviews the application and ensures it meets underwriting guidelines.

3. The underwriter validates the application and obtains information (for example, a DMV report).

4. The underwriter assigns the risk score, prices accordingly based on score, policy limits, deductible, and so on; produces a quote; and forwards it to the agent.

5. The agent presents the quote and obtains an agreement from the policyholder.

6. The underwriter issues the policy and premium billing and sends this to the agent.

7. The policyholder remits the premium payment.

Extensions:

- Application information is incomplete

  - Underwriter requests missing information

  - Agent obtains missing information from applicant

- Applicant rejects initial quote due to price

  - Underwriter rerates using higher deductible

  - Applicant accepts new quote

- Applicant conceals information on application

  - Underwriter declines application

  - Underwriter probes to determine if application willfully concealed and whether agent was party to any concealment/misrepresentation

Variations:

- Applicant is a member of a group (employer, college alumna, or professional association); additional discounts may apply in pricing

- Applicant has other policies with insurance company; additional discounts may apply in pricing

- Payment is requested in installments versus single payment; billing and accounting changes required

- Additional driver or vehicle requested to be added to policy; additional underwriting information and review required

A fourth and emerging business requirements definition approach is **Dimensional Analysis.** In this approach, the data is analyzed into metrics or measures (amounts, counts, and so on) and into dimensions or facts (time, organization, geography, product, and channel) by subject area (for example, underwriting, claims, and so on) and then analyzed to determine which business objectives the data can support (see Figure 3-2).

This is a bottom-up approach derived from the data to the analysis versus a top-down approach like the **Analytic Actionability Framework.** Dimensional Analysis had been referred to as "letting the data speak for itself." This is useful when business users have difficulty in defining their business objectives and/or business questions. Instead of asking what business questions they need to answer, the analyst reviews the data with them and asks what business problems that data can help address.

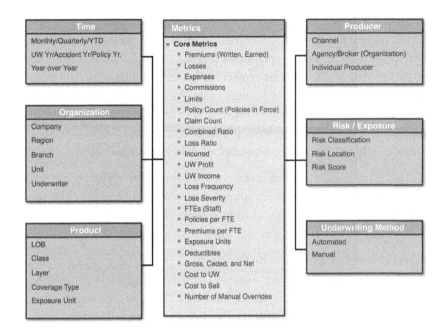

Figure 3-2 Underwriting Dimensional Analysis Example

After requirements are defined, regardless of the approach used, analytic initiatives and projects need to be prioritized to rationalize limited resources and to build effective roadmaps. The prioritization is based on two key factors. The first is the projected value to business; the value should be defined during the business requirements process. Requirements with the highest value are usually associated with strategy corporate initiatives, regulatory compliance, mergers and acquisitions, market and competitive capabilities, and profitability or revenue growth. The second aspect is the feasibility of delivering the analytic request based on data and information. Factors that influence feasabilty are granularity and dimensionality, degree of manual intervention (or data acquisition and matching) and ease of access to the information. These two dimensions should be defined as part of every analytic project request. The need and value for some analytic requests may be so obvious that not much documentation needs to done; for example, they are truly "table stakes" or basic foundational capabilities.

With this information, IT reviews overall business needs in the aggregate across all business units to rank initiatives and build an overall analytic roadmap. Many organizations leverage user steering committees as part of this process. Often projects of less than 90 days just get added to a queue. Larger ones are subject to committee review. IT also often looks at common capabilities needed across business units and needs to deliver new tools. IT also looks at data sources needed across business areas to help prioritize data sourcing or data governance efforts.

Unlike traditional transactional system projects, which use a waterfall system development life cycle approach, analytics projects are assumed to be iterative. They are delivered in shorter "spurts" and are presumed to have additional enhancements.

Figure 3-3 shows a classic 2 by 2 matrix used to visualize and prioritize value versus feasibility using common underwriting analytic objectives as a business unit prioritization example. In practice, an organization would be looking at requests across business areas and would drill down into the data sources needed across them and capabilities (for example, tools or training) needed across units as well.

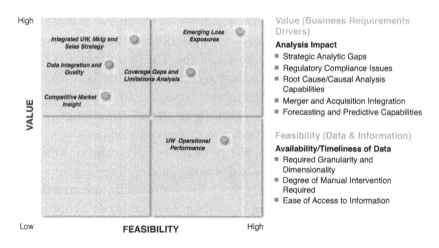

Figure 3-3 Prioritization Matrix for Underwriting

Alignment

Alignment is sought on two levels. The first is strategic alignment. As part of long-term and annual corporate strategy and planning processes, each business area defines strategic initiatives, which support corporate strategy and initiatives. This is one form of alignment.

A second level of alignment is peer alignment across business units. Not all analytic requirements can be addressed immediately. The initiatives need to be plotted based on value to the business and feasibility. An executive steering committee typically makes the final determination as to what initiatives get delivered, based on feedback and recommendations from a working committee. But it is also important that other stakeholders within the organization including the management team, the IT BI development team, and individual contributors like data stewards and business analysts are part of the process and aware of the rationale for the prioritization.

This communication process is termed alignment and is part of the overall BI strategy governance. This helps people understand why their request or initiatives may be delivered later than wanted, based on the greater good for the organization. These committees and stakeholders are a part of the organization and governance processes, which are reviewed in more detail in Chapter 8, "Organization and Implementation."

Summary

Learning Objectives

Test your basic knowledge of the main points in this chapter by answering the following questions:

- Compare various methods used to define analytic business requirements.

- Review the process and factors used to prioritize analytic projects/initiatives.

- Understand the importance of alignment and how it is conducted within an organization.

Discussion Questions

Further check your application of key concepts by reviewing the following discussion questions:

- Discuss two approaches that can be used to define analytic business requirements.

- Name three factors that typically drive business value. Name three factors related to data that affect feasibility.

Key Terms

Business discovery refers to the process used to derive business requirements for business intelligence or analytics. Typically done through a facilitated interview by a business analyst asking questions to discover current gaps and future needs, align them to or across departmental and corporate strategies and assess the potential value of the stated needs.

Dimensions are attributes or characteristics related to metrics; typically include organization, geography, product, and time. Usually have a hierarchy or levels of detail, for example, group, company, department, and unit.

Metrics are financial measures; can be counts, amounts, percentages, and so on. Are subcomponents of Key Performance Indicators (KPIs) that are strategic metrics used in corporate performance management. Can be classified as leading metrics or indicators, which "drive" KPIs.

Scenario refers to paths from trigger events to goals as part of a Use Case.

Use Cases refer to a set of interactions in a situation for a specific goal. Include a combination of scenarios with different roles or actors involved in the business process for a goal. Often used in BIs to validate user interfaces and process flows.

Additional Resources/Reading:

Cockburn, *Writing Effective Use Cases*. Addison-Wesley. 2001.

4

Defining and Using Metrics Effectively

Business performance is managed and measured in quantifiable terms, generically referred to as metrics. Business Performance Management (BPM), also referred to as Corporate Performance Management (CPM), encompasses all the processes, information, and systems used to set strategy; develops plans; monitors their execution; forecasts performance; and reports results. It includes strategic planning, tactical planning; budgeting and planning; forecasting; financial planning; activity-based costing (ABC) and profitability analysis; management reporting; and governance, risk and compliance (GRC) management. Many of these processes are supported by integrated Enterprise Performance Management (EPM) or Governance Risk and Compliance (GRC) analytics applications. Regardless if integrated or siloed or the degree of automation, a critical success factor in all these related processes is defining and measuring the right metrics and using them consistently across processes. Metrics are part of business requirements but need to be used consistently. Data governance discussed in Chapter 6, "Data and Information Architecture," plays a key role in defining, documenting, and communicating metrics for consistency.

Metric Types

There is much confusion on metrics versus *Key Performance Indicators (KPIs)*, *leading indicators*, *lagging indicators*, and *drivers*. All KPIs are metrics but not all metrics are KPIs. Metrics can measure anything, but KPIs measure what matters most. KPIs are the end resulting metric, for example, Loss Ratio or Combined Ratio. Organizations can have many metrics but should have few KPIs. KPIs should be actionable or you cannot achieve your goals. This is why the **Analytic Actionability Matrix** reviewed in Chapter 3, "Defining, Prioritizing, and Aligning Needs," is valuable; it provides a framework to associate KPIs and metrics with each objective to validate its actionability. Effective KPIs have two main characteristics: They are *outcome-oriented*, meaning they are tied to an objective or business goal; they are *target-based*, meaning they are associated with a one-time-based target value.

Leading indicators look forward and forecast future performance and provide insight into areas that are still actionable, for example, (Claims) Days to Contact. They are often submetrics of a KPI. The value of leading indicators is in monitoring them and taking actions that influence the target KPI while you can still affect its outcome. **Drivers** are a form of a leading indicator; they are often external metrics that affect internal performance. For example, the Consumer Price Index might drive Labor Rates, which are part of Losses Incurred.

Lagging indicators look backward and provide a view of performance to date; they are often financial, for example, Loss Ratio. They are KPI-related metrics but cannot affect current or future performance, as they are after the act, but they can provide insight into root cause analysis that can help future performance.

Metric Visualization

Metrics are critical to managing business performance; aligning and focusing attention on them and tying them to wanted performance outcomes helps align the organization with policyholders, shareholders, partners, and regulators. To manage performance effectively, everyone in the organization must have visibility to them. The most common ways to provide this visibility are through scorecards and dashboards. Additional visualization tools will be discussed further in Chapter 7, "Analytics Tools."

The **Balanced Score Card (BSC)** is an enterprise performance management approach that covers four key metric areas or perspectives. Following are the questions these perspectives address and metric focus areas:

- **Financial:** To succeed, what must we communicate to our shareholders?

Metric focus: profitability, growth, and shareholder value

- **Customer:** To achieve our strategies, what must we measure for customer satisfaction?

Metric focus: Time, quality, services, and price/cost

- **Operational/process:** To satisfy our customers, what business processes must we excel at?

Metric focus: Time, quality, productivity, and cost

- **Employee/people:** To achieve our strategies, how must our organization function?

Metric focus: Innovation, education and training, and intellectual assets

Scorecards can be used at the corporate, divisional/departmental, and individual levels. Figure 4-1 shows an example of the corporate level and an example of an Insurance Balanced Score Card.

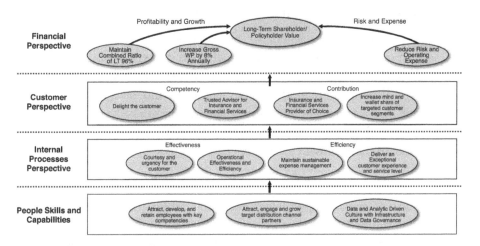

Mission: Be the preferred insurance and financial services organization of choice for our customers, partners, shareholders and employees.

Figure 4-1 Insurance Company Balanced Score Card Example

Dashboards, sometimes also called management cockpits, tend to be more tactical and often more process or functionally related. They are less defined as to perspective or content than Balanced Score Cards (BSCs). They can include "widgets" like speedometers and slider bars for "what if" or simple scenario analysis. They also typically have drill-down capability and links to ad hoc reports for root cause analysis.

Figure 4-2 shows a Property and Casualty Insurance Income Statement dashboard. This dashboard could be used standalone or could be included as part of a composite dashboard or set of dashboards.

On the top of the dashboard, you can see a metric tree showing the calculation of pretax income from left to right. Note the KPIs Loss Ratio, Expense Ratio, and Combined Ratio, all the way to the right below Pretax Income. The Pretax Income KPI component metrics, or decomposition, from left to right are also shown: Earned Premium (and its submetrics Written Premium – Renewal and Written Premium – New Business), Investment Income, Claims Incurred, Total Operating Expenses (and its submetrics, Commissions and Other Operating Expenses) are shown in the top half of the dashboard.

In the lower half of the dashboard, the leading indicators or drivers are shown with sliders that provide the "what If" or simple scenario analysis. If new business growth rate increases, the written premium, earned premium, and pretax income also increases.

Figure 4-3 shows how dashboards can effectively be designed to support sales in insurance using metric tree analysis and metric decomposition. It starts by defining core sales metrics and three supporting metric areas or processes: Sales Financials, Sales Operations and Sales Staffing, and the sub metrics for each. These three main tactics can be further decomposed into three separate dashboards. Also note the (Sales) Executive Dashboard metrics that could be developed into a fourth dashboard for Sales Summary. In a design session you would define Use Cases by role (Sales VP, Sales Manager, Sales Representative) and navigation patterns with key metrics each would see on their dashboard. You would also develop the visualization of the metrics including targets, performance to date versus targets and variance, past performance, time dimensionality, key related metrics, and so on. But one of the critical requirements and design tools is the metric tree approach.

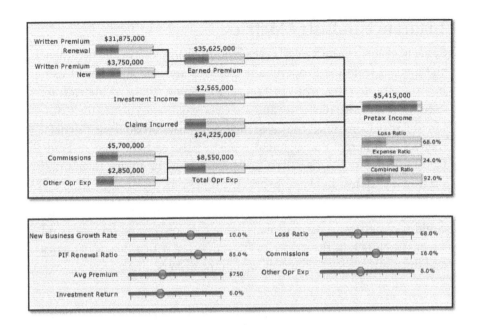

Figure 4-2 Property and Casualty Income Statement Dashboard

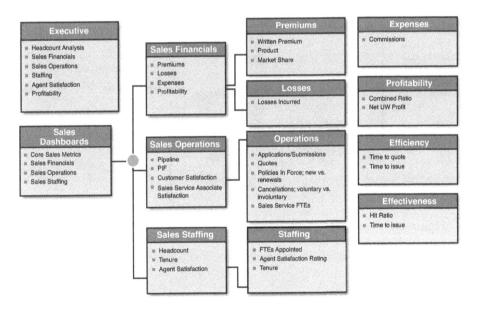

Figure 4-3 Insurance Sales Metric Framework

Insurance Industry Metrics

Some insurance industry KPIs are obvious; examples include the financial metrics from the Property and Casualty Income Statement Dashboard example referred to in Figure 4-2. Some financial metrics are used for regulatory reporting and are clearly defined, such as the Combined Ratio. Companies may also include a variation on these financial metrics for internal management reporting use as well, such as Trade Combined Ratio. Further, there are metrics that are unique to an organization's business model or to specific functions.

Figure 4.4 shows how a Property and Casualty Insurance Company could use metrics to drive growth using two key levers: revenues and expenses. Note how the strategies are supported with a variety of tactics and the metrics KPIs for each as well as the drivers.

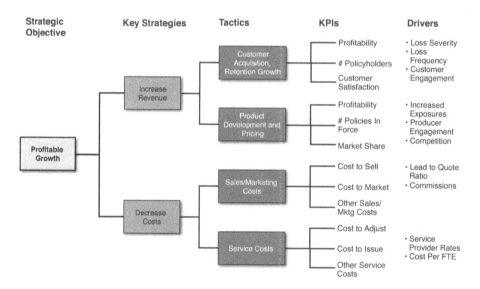

Figure 4-4 Profitable Growth KPIs—Metrics and Drivers

There are a number of commonly used metrics by business function. Figure 4-5 shows some of the most common ones.

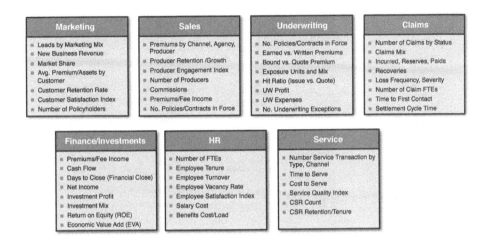

Marketing	Sales	Underwriting	Claims
▪ Leads by Marketing Mix ▪ New Business Revenue ▪ Market Share ▪ Avg. Premium/Assets by Customer ▪ Customer Retention Rate ▪ Customer Satisfaction Index ▪ Number of Policyholders	▪ Premiums by Channel, Agency, Producer ▪ Producer Retention /Growth ▪ Producer Engagement Index ▪ Number of Producers ▪ Commissions ▪ Premiums/Fee Income ▪ No. Policies/Contracts in Force	▪ No. Policies/Contracts in Force ▪ Earned vs. Written Premiums ▪ Bound vs. Quote Premium ▪ Exposure Units and Mix ▪ Hit Ratio (Issue vs. Quote) ▪ UW Profit ▪ UW Expenses ▪ No. Underwriting Exceptions	▪ Number of Claims by Status ▪ Claims Mix ▪ Incurred, Reserves, Paids ▪ Recoveries ▪ Loss Frequency, Severity ▪ Number of Claim FTEs ▪ Time to First Contact ▪ Settlement Cycle Time

Finance/Investments	HR	Service
▪ Premiums/Fee Income ▪ Cash Flow ▪ Days to Close (Financial Close) ▪ Net Income ▪ Investment Profit ▪ Investment Mix ▪ Return on Equity (ROE) ▪ Economic Value Add (EVA)	▪ Number of FTEs ▪ Employee Tenure ▪ Employee Turnover ▪ Employee Vacancy Rate ▪ Employee Satisfaction Index ▪ Salary Cost ▪ Benefits Cost/Load	▪ Number Service Transaction by Type, Channel ▪ Time to Serve ▪ Cost to Serve ▪ Service Quality Index ▪ CSR Count ▪ CSR Retention/Tenure

Figure 4-5 Common Insurance Metrics by Function

Metric Maturity

Metrics use and maturity vary from company to company; the granularity and ability to define, measure, and manage by metrics is an evolution (see Figure 4-6). Typically the top financial metrics are well understood within an organization. Conflicting issues arise due to departmental metric definition or use when different departments define a metric in their own terms or when they use a common metric but call it another name. This data management issue must be addressed through data governance, which is covered in more detail in Chapter 6.

Mature organizations use metric frameworks and methodologies to decompose metrics and measure them via dashboards.

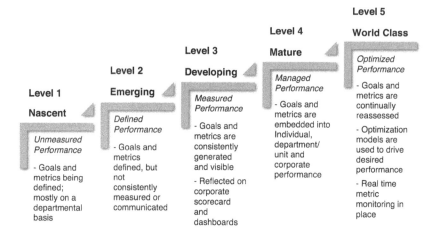

Figure 4-6 Metric Maturity Model

Summary

Learning Objectives

Test your basic knowledge of the main points in this chapter by answering the following questions:

- Understand the importance and role of metrics in business performance management and BI requirements.

- Compare various metric types and various metric visualization options.

- Apply metric definition and metric maturity frameworks.

- Review examples of common insurance industry metrics.

Discussion Questions

Further check your application of key concepts by reviewing the following discussion questions:

- Describe differences between KPIs, leading indicators, and lagging indicators.

- Give an example of two metrics used to measure profitable growth in insurance. Give two of each for revenue and for expenses.

- Give an example of a KPI and related supporting metrics used in sales for sales financial, sales operations, and sales staffing management.

Key Terms

Drivers are a form of leading indicator; they are often external metrics that affect internal performance. For example, the minimum wage could drive labor rates.

Key Performance Indicators (KPIs) are metrics that measure what matters most. Metrics can measure anything, but KPIs are the end resulting metric. Organizations can have many metrics but should have few KPIs.

Leading indicators are metrics that look forward and forecast future performance. They provide insight into areas that are still actionable.

Lagging indicators are metrics that look backward and provide a view of performance to date; they are often financial, for example, Loss Ratio. They are KPI-related metrics but cannot affect current or past performance because they are after the act, but they can provide insight into root cause analysis that can help future performance.

Additional Resources/Reading

ACORD Framework Business Glossary includes definitions and characteristics for key data elements and metric used in the Property and Casualty and Life and Annuity industries developed by the working committees within ACORD. www.acord.org.

Parmenter, David. *Key Performance Indicators.* Wiley & Sons. 2010.

Olve, Nils-Goran, et al. *Performance Drivers: A Practice Guide to Using the Balanced Scorecard.* Wiley & Sons. 1999.

Deloitte Enterprise Value Map is a one-page tool that shows the relationship between shareholder value and business operations. An insurance industry-specific enterprise value map is also available. Search for

Enterprise Value Map and see the white paper, "The Value Habit: A Practical Guide to Creating Value" at www.deloitte.com.

Global Environmental Management Initiative (GEMI) Metrics Navigator™ is a tool to help organizations develop and implement metrics that provide insight into complex issues, support business strategy, and contribute to business success. The tool presents a six-step process to select, implement, and evaluate a set of "critical few" metrics that focus on an organization's success. It includes worksheets, a series of questions, or checklists for each step. (Note: Although GEMI is focused on environmental sustainability, the metrics tools are excellent and apply across industries and processes.) www.gemi.org/metricsnavigator/.

5

Analytics Value and
Return on Investment

The business value of analytics, and how to determine value, has been a key element of strategic BI programs and analytics champions. According to a study by Nucleus Research, if the median Fortune 1,000 businesses increased their usability of data by just 10%, there would be an annual revenue increase of $2.0 billion. In the same study the firm stated that there is a 1,000% ROI for organizations that do make analytic investments. This projection is a bit aggressive for the insurance industry in which analytics are widely used; yet analytics are often stove-piped creating additional opportunities if integrated. Even one-half of this projection is a significant opportunity in the industry.

The spotlight on analytics continues to shine especially in light of increased expectations driven by *"Big Data"* and "Internet of Everything." Big Data is about leveraging the explosion of data created by mobile devices, social media, and machine generated data, such as jet engines, medical devices, and so on. The three Vs of Big Data are Volume, Variety (traditional structured, new unstructured data like text from social media, machine produced, and so on), and Velocity (the rapidity of change in the data and the value of acting on data in real time); the 4th V of Big Data and perhaps least touted but most significant V is Value. *The Internet of Everything* refers to the interconnection of analytics and things that use them such as bar codes, RFID tags, computers in cars, mobile phones, and such, where the things gain context awareness, increased processing power, and greater sensing abilities.

Analytics in insurance have been providing value but have largely been limited to siloed application areas, for example, sales channel and producer performance management, underwriting performance, claims management, marketing analysis and actuarial pricing, or reserving analysis. The value of analytics within each of these "silos" is often visible and quite mature, but their impact and contribution to the business is relatively immature from an enterprise perspective due to the lack of an integrated enterprise approach. Therefore, integrating analytics across these domains and understanding the value, leverage, and correlations between them is still a rich area of opportunity. Organizations can realize this greater value by adopting a *value management approach*, which is a methodical approach to measure and manage value. However, culture and change management are two significant hurdles to be overcome as business users will naturally focus on their own departmental interests. These hurdles can best be addressed by incorporating value management best practices and institutionalizing them in Business Intelligence Competency Centers (BICCs).

Business Challenges

The insurance industry faces huge challenges as it consolidates and as new nontraditional competitors enter the market. Monitoring customer engagement, which leads to retention and growth, is a key challenge for all industry segments due to the barrage of 24/7 always-on communication channels. A similar challenge exists for producer engagement and agency management in distinguishing your products from your competitors'. Health insurers are under significant challenges under the recent U.S. ObamaCare law to make sure that more of the premium dollar is spent on actual medical loss costs and to focus on wellness and disease management efforts that reduce risk. In response, insurers are developing new business models to drive profitability and market share; they are using data and analytics as key capabilities.

Insurers must take a value-driven approach to analytics, one that states the value of analytics in the terms of the business or face a lack of sustained funding. Insurers have many competing requests for limited financial and people resources. All too often investments in analytics are overridden in favor of operational or transactional systems such as marketing campaign management, policy or contract management, agency and sales management, claims management, finance and accounting systems, and the like.

Even when analytics are addressed, all too often they are focused on operational analytics embedded within these transactional or operational systems such as reports of overdue accounts receivables or upcoming policy renewals. Analytics that span these transactional systems and can bring greater enterprise value get short shrift. Organizations fail to realize that classic back-end analytics make their operational systems more effective and smarter because they identify key opportunity areas.

Following are three key types of Business Intelligence: strategic, tactical, and operational BI.

- **Strategic BI** is used to manage strategic or long-term business plans and goals. Executives and senior management use KPIs to monitor how the business is actually performing against strategic goals such as market share, premium growth, expense reduction, or underwriting profitability.

- **Tactical BI** is used to monitor and manage business initiatives or tactics that support strategic performance. They are used by senior management, functional managers, and business analysts to measure performance and develop or refine tactics to meet goals. Note that some tactical analytics have been packaged into separate analytic applications such as campaign management, fraud management, and risk management.

- **Operational BI** is used to analyze and manage transactional or operational business processes on a daily or even real-time basis in areas such as underwriting, claim management, policyholder/member service, billing, and so on. An example would be a list of open claims or a list of policies due to expire within 60 days, or reviewing the list of current calls waiting in a call center queue.

Figure 5-1 shows how these different types of BI are used and relate to one another.

Area: Strategic Planning
Focus: Strategic Objectives
Action: Monitor/Report Results

Area: Tactical Planning
Focus: Tactics, Initiatives
Action: Develop/Adjust Tactics

Area: Operational Plans
Focus: Resource Allocation
Action: Analyze Results/Report
Variances

Figure 5-1 Strategic Versus Tactical Versus Operational BI

Therefore, it is critical that organizations have an analytic strategy that is business-driven, is strategically aligned, and shows value. This value-based approach keeps focus on choosing the right projects clearly driving ownership and accountability for business results and delivery on commitments for these results. Communicating successful projects with proven value will ensure ongoing funding. Unfortunately, most organizations have not demonstrated compelling value propositions so far largely because they lack an end-to-end value-based approach to analytics, a full-value life cycle, or a Value-Based Management approach, as shown in Figure 5-2 where value measurement and management fits into the overall BI strategy.

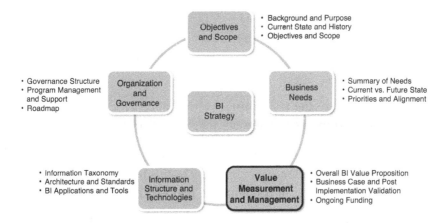

Figure 5-2 BI Strategy Framework

Value-Based Management

Business owners need to make their analytics needs known to their IT partners, to express them in the context of their business imperatives to get their share of analytics funding, and to help make sure that IT gets analytics funded adequately. This starts during the annual planning and budgeting process when the business submits requests for resources. Any significant project will require a business case to obtain resources and for development prioritization. Following successful implementation of a project, the business and IT should also engage in a "value realization" analysis that documents the actual value attained from the analytics project. Organizations can use the value realization not only to communicate successful results, but also to ensure ongoing and "cascading" funding to support future initiatives.

A Value-Based Management approach to this value life cycle has three phases: Discovery - Investing for impact; Realization - Delivering business outcomes; and Optimization - Governing ongoing performance.

The following describes these three phases in more detail.

- Value Discovery develops a value-based business strategy and business case, enabled by technology and aligned with corporate objectives. It answers these questions:

- What are our business imperatives and how do you align your business and IT strategy?

- What is the expected impact to address these imperatives (business cases)?

- What are the right initiatives to address the value creation opportunities and how are they prioritized?

- Value Realization develops transformational strategies to mobilize, deliver, and measure business results based on insights into leading practices or benchmarks. It answers these questions:

  - How should we prioritize, mobilize, and govern programs to deliver value?

  - How can the business case be made actionable at the operating level and how is value measured?

  - How should we govern, architect, deploy, and ensure quality of master data?

  - How can we govern, architect, and set up an information framework for business analytics?

- Value Optimization assesses how the implementation and program compares to best or leading practices and recommends areas in which the business can drive more value from current investments. Key questions addressed in this phase are

  - What is the value realized by our program and how can we derive even more value from existing investments?

  - What insights do we have regarding the total cost of ownership?

  - How does our implementation compare to best or leading practices?

  - How can we utilize a periodic business process like a "health check" to continuously measure our progress internally as well as against industry peers or other industry analytics leaders?

- How can we mobilize and govern a program to optimize success?

- What services make sense in a shared service center, and what is the right approach to setting up these shared services for maximum value measurement efficiency and effectiveness?

Figure 5-3 summarizes the value life cycle components.

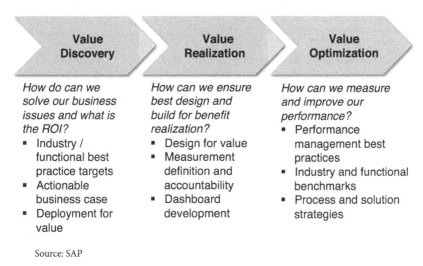

Value Discovery	Value Realization	Value Optimization
How do can we solve our business issues and what is the ROI?	*How can we ensure best design and build for benefit realization?*	*How can we measure and improve our performance?*
• Industry / functional best practice targets	• Design for value	• Performance management best practices
• Actionable business case	• Measurement definition and accountability	• Industry and functional benchmarks
• Deployment for value	• Dashboard development	• Process and solution strategies

Source: SAP

Figure 5-3 Value Life Cycle

SAP is a major global software vendor well known for enterprise accounting software and is a thought leader in Value-Based Management. Industry and cross-industry benchmarks and a Value Based Management Institute are capabilities offered through the Americas SAP User Group (ASUG), which is run by SAP customers. More than 10,000 companies, both SAP customers and noncustomers, have participated in more than 30 business process benchmark surveys with almost 600 participating in Business Intelligence specific surveys.

Research based on participation by this group has shown that high adopters of a value management-based approach achieve significantly more value than low adopters. These high adopter companies deliver twice as many projects on time and on budget, and show more than 1.5 times greater value than low adopters, regardless of industry.

Insurance Analytics Value Framework: Key Drivers

Four key value driver areas are used to increase overall financial business performance, or profitability, in insurance:

- **Revenue growth:**

    - Volume metrics measure policyholders/customer and policies per policyholder/customer (penetration), as well as existing customer retention and growth.

    - Price metrics evaluate increased premiums per policy/contract, policyholder/member/household as well as improved profitability per product or policyholder/member/household.

- **Operating margin:**

    - General and Administrative (G&A) Expenses metrics measure improving customer/member/policyholder interaction cost efficiency and improving administrative service efficiency especially in HR and IT.

    - Cost of Service metrics used to improve policy and claims service costs and overall delivery efficiency.

    - Cost of Sales metrics used to measure producer acquisition and training costs, commissions and other sales incentives, and producer management service costs.

- **Asset efficiency:**

    - Service Provider metrics measure improving service effectiveness and efficiency including provider vendor management and leakage such as appraisers, inspectors, lawyers, physicians/other medical providers.

    - Premium and Non-Premium Receivables and Payables Management metrics improve receivables and payables efficiency, for example, Percent of Bad Debt, Percent of Late Charges, Percent of Accounts Receivables unbilled, and so on.

- **Organizational Effectiveness:**

  - Organizational Strength metrics focus on improving agement and governance effectiveness (for example, bus. planning, business performance management) and improving execution capabilities (for example, operational excellence, agility and flexibility, and strategic assets).

  - External Factors metrics include key macro or micro economic KPIs such as unemployment rate, and so on.

These value areas can be applied to three key business performance categories: Underwriting Performance, Operational Performance, and Finance Performance, as shown in Figure 5-4. Each of these key performance areas has several key business value opportunity areas in which analytics can be applied.

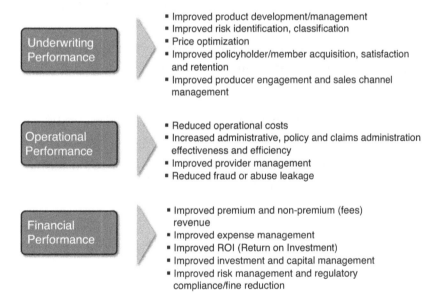

Figure 5-4 Insurance Performance Management Business Objectives

BI Performance Opportunities and Benchmarks for IT

In addition to direct revenue and expense impacts from the business, insurance organizations can also measure and improve their BI IT capabilities and overall performance in supporting the business.

IT can also contribute to justifying analytic investments based on reducing Total Cost of Ownership (TCO) including software acquisition (license) costs, software maintenance costs, administrative support costs, help desk support, and end user training costs. IT TCO is only part of the value picture; the strategic business case for investment must include business revenue and expense components, as well as IT TCO.

After analytic investments have been approved and made, benchmarking is an effective way to measure performance both against internal best performance, and against external best in class not only in insurance or financial services but also across all industries.

Specific BI related objectives and related KPIs as part of an effective BI Performance Analytics program include:

- **Effectiveness**
    - Usage of BI by employees, executives, and external stakeholders (BI adoption)
    - Level of insights generated through BI usage by the business process (BI maturity)

- **Efficiency**
    - BI project mix (for example, reports, dashboards, and semantic views)
    - Cycle times, reliability, and uptime
    - BI costs

- **BI technology**
    - BI technology leveraged for analytics, data warehousing, and data management

- **Organization**
  - BI Organization Model
  - Level of centralization
  - Size of support organization
- **Best practices adoption**
  - Importance of best practices
  - Current coverage of best practices
  - Importance and coverage gap

BICCs can start tracking and comparing their historical performance and publish an internal scorecard for transparency. They can also participate in an external benchmarking survey and add comparative benchmarks to their scorecards. Insurers can participate in various BI benchmarking surveys. Two well-known ones are available from SAP and TDWI (The Data Warehousing Institute).

Using BI Competency Centers to Institutionalize Value

BICCs can ensure that value management is part of every project and institutionalize it in an organization's overall BI program. Organizations have been forming BI Competency Centers (or Centers of Excellence, aka BI CoEs) to leverage best practices and improve operational effectiveness and efficiency to ensure business user satisfaction and demonstrate BI value.

BICCs play a key role in defining and executing an organization's BI strategy especially in demonstrating and communicating the value of analytics. They have responsibility for several key areas of the strategy including the development, documentation, and communication of the organization's overall BI strategy; development of the business requirements for a project and prioritizing all projects; defining the business case for each project and identifying supporting capabilities; defining an information taxonomy, architecture, and managing the technology tools; and lastly managing the governance, program management, roadmap, measurement, training and support. See more about BICCs in Chapter 8, "Organization and Implementation."

Two key emerging roles that support value management within a BICC, are KPI analyst and value analyst. The **KPI analyst** helps define key performance indicators, leading indicators, and correlation metrics in the design phase. The **value analyst** helps define the anticipated ROI for the business case and validates attained ROI in the post-implementation value assessment. In smaller organizations these functions are often also conducted by a business analyst who can reside in the BICC or in business units. In larger organizations a value analyst may be part of a Performance Management function in the Finance (for example, Activity Based Costing) or Corporate Strategy areas. KPI analysts, value analysts, and business analysts all play a key role in the business benefit area of the BI Strategy Framework.

A third role that contributes to value management and communication of value is the **communication analyst**; this developing role can help broadcast analytic successes including quantitative value. Communications analysts are often part of the Education and Training function within the organization area of the BI Strategy Framework. These roles are part of the Organization and Governance component of the BI Strategy Framework, as part of Program Management Support (see Chapter 8).

Business Performance-Based Approach to Value

Using a value-based approach is a shift from a simple "on time and on budget" method to a business outcomes and value-based one. Many companies have focused on reducing IT and administrative costs that are important but have far less impact on the business than revenue opportunities. Analytic-driven companies adopt a broader performance management approach and develop the following strategies and accountabilities:

- They demand that IT investments deliver competitive advantage.
- They focus change on high-impact results.
- They set ambitious business goals enabled by equally ambitious talent.
- They drive accountability through measurement.
- They embrace a culture of performance obsession.

Following are leading practices used to actualize value management:

- **Performance improvement:** Organizations consistently and proactively measure and compare themselves internally and externally to identify new opportunities to gain more value from business processes

- **Justification:** Organizations have a formal process to justify investments that involve stakeholders across the business.

- **Value realization:** During project implementations, organizations design the solution to realize the value identified in the business case. They develop a key performance improvement framework, complete with clearly identified ownership and accountability.

- **Business strategy–IT alignment:** Business process leads and IT professionals collaborate on everything from strategic planning to program execution to ensure that their objectives are well aligned.

- **Governance and portfolio management:** Executive leadership is engaged to help ensure project success.

- **Organizational excellence:** Programs are staffed and managed by a talented team that is measured based on the quantifiable business value its programs achieve.

The change management required to shift to this approach should not be underestimated. However, the return in terms of analytics value recognition and sustained funding that enable insurers to be truly analytics-driven and show direct benefit to business performance, well justifies their efforts required.

Summary

Learning Objectives

Test your basic knowledge of the main points in this chapter by answering the following questions:

- Review the need for determining the value of analytics both for overall strategic funding and individual project justification.

- Understand the value life cycle components.

- Compare the various revenue and expense value areas and potential performance impact areas in insurance.

- Describe elements of IT Total Cost of Ownership.

Discussion Questions

Further check your application of key concepts by reviewing the following discussion questions:

- Discuss three components of a value management approach.

- Identify four value opportunity areas.

- Name three performance management impact areas.

- Describe the differences between strategic, tactical, and operational BI.

Key Terms

Big Data refers to people, processes, and technologies employed in leveraging the explosion of data created by mobile devices, social media, and machine-generated data, such as jet engines, medical devices, and so on. The three Vs of Big Data are Volume, Variety (traditional structured, new unstructured data like text from social media, machine produced, and so on.), and Velocity (the rapidity of change in the data and the value of acting on data in real time). Big Data technologies encompass the full spectrum of analytics technologies including information management, database management, and analytics.

Value Management Approach refers to a methodical approach used to measure and manage value for initial business case value validation as well as post implementation value realization.

Additional Resources/Reading

ASUG-SAP Benchmarking Forum is a facility to exchange metrics and best practices. Covers 26 business processes with 2,600 participants over 1,400 companies including healthcare organizations. The BI survey has been conducted since 2007. Participation is free and open to both SAP and non-SAP customers. https://valuemanagement.sap.com/# or http://www.asug.com/benchmarking.

HIMSS (Health Information & Management Systems Society) www.himss.org HIMSS Analytics and the International Institute for Analytics (IIA) www.iianalytics.com have partnered to create the DELTA-Powered (Healthcare) Analytics Assessment, a new maturity model that assesses and scores the analytical capabilities of healthcare organizations. This survey and certification program provides a roadmap to gauge how organizations leverage data and analytics. http://www.himssanalytics.org/emram/delta.aspx

TDWI (The Data Warehouse Institute) www.tdwi.org is a leading educational and research organization for BI and Data Warehousing. TDWI produces an annual *BI Benchmark Report.*

6

Data and Information Architecture

Data is a corporate asset but to get the most value out of data, it needs to be stored, managed, and accessible. Data and information architecture are critical to access your data. Without it, you don't know what data means or you create data that is hidden and isn't leveraged for insight.

The process of organizing data, defining the processes to collect, and store and use data are the responsibility of data architects. The governance and strategy of information processes and how they create value, protecting this value as a whole including compliance and strategic impact is referred to as information architecture.

To be usable, business (or logical versus physical) views of the data must be defined and built to organize the data that is created from multiple transactional systems. These views on the data and the business processes are needed for the analytics to the business. These views should be built by information technology based on requirements from business owners. Business leadership is critical for effective information architecture because only business leaders understand the organization's real information and business process needs. This leadership is provided through the *data governance* process and related committees.

Insurance companies have spent millions of dollars building data repositories that did not effectively meet end user information needs. Users could not find the information they needed easily or on a timely basis. These data warehouse or data marts and related business intelligence programs often failed due to a lack of executive sponsorship and financial support, a lack of planning, poor data quality or understandability, and ineffective access to the data. Essentially, they failed because of a lack of ongoing alignment and engagement with the business.

To address these challenges an *enterprise information architecture* and standards, supported by data dictionaries, data quality programs, and data governance are essential. Business engagement in these areas is absolutely critical. The purpose of this chapter is to help executives and end business users gain an overall understanding of data and information architecture and their roles and responsibilities in these areas.

Corporate strategy drives information strategy. An organization's business model and strategic plan and objectives should drive the organization's *information strategy*. Priorities and investments in information architecture and related data governance activities should follow the business strategy.

Data and information architecture addresses the way your data is organized, how it is integrated from multiple sources, how access is provided, how it is governed, how it is consumed, and how to ensure data quality. Lack of an information strategy, which includes data and information architecture, is also one of the key causes of the lack of analytics adoption. Data understandability is often perceived as a data quality issue; users do not understand the data definition, its source of origin, and its intended use or any "nuances" in the data. As a result, they create their own data sets compounding existing data fragmentation and data confusion.

Data includes not only the structured data in underwriting, claims, customer/member, agency/producer management, and financial systems, but also the unstructured data from claim adjusting notes, X-rays, photographs, and diagrams attached to claims and underwriting files, web logs, social media, call center notes, and more. As these data assets grow and data types increase in diversity, it becomes even more challenging to store, connect, and provide timely and useful access to data in an efficient and cost-effective way. A formalized information or data strategy as a component of an overall BI or analytics strategy is imperative, as shown in Figure 6-1.

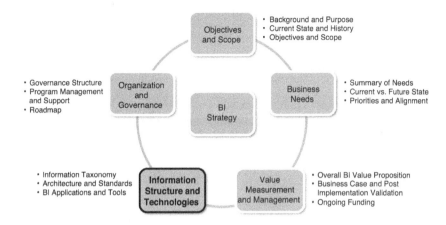

Figure 6-1 BI Strategy Framework

Information Strategy Framework

An information strategy framework is part of the overall BI or analytic strategy framework. It is part of the information structure and technologies area and includes five key elements:

Access: Information retrieval methods needed to provide effective information access

Includes: Search methodologies, analytics, navigation design, and user interface

Business role: Requirements definition

Generation: Processes to extract, integrate, and create information from raw data

Includes: Systems interfaces, automated extraction programs, business rules to harmonize data, and calculate KPIs

Business role: Requirements definition and testing

Organization: Categorizes and provides a roadmap to data

Incudes: Data modeling, data structures, classification, metadata (data about data), and semantics

Business role: Requirements definition and data stewardship

Governance: Processes and business rules to ensure data quality and consistency

Includes: Information stewardship, master data management, and policy conformance

Business role: Data stewardship and business rules definition

Service: Processes and policies needed to preserve overall data service quality

Includes: Data security, quality, reliability, scalability, and usefulness

Business role: Data security and retention requirements

Figure 6-2 illustrates these five elements with the questions they answer on the left and the related component on the right.

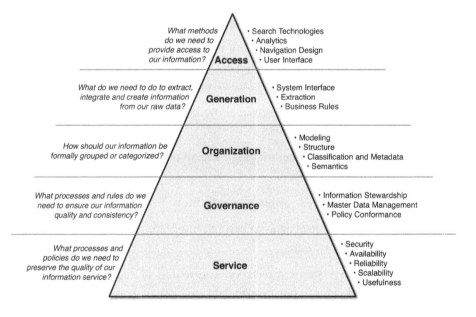

Figure 6-2 Information Strategy Framework

Insurance Information Taxonomy

A *Taxonomy* is an information categorization framework agreed upon by business and content stewards used to tag or categorize content.

Think back to sixth-grade science where you learned the Linnaean taxonomy of animal, vegetable, or mineral. It organizes and provides a roadmap to the data. Taxonomies can be used for many purposes; the key one covered in this chapter is for analytics. Taxonomies have also been created for reporting purposes such as extended business reporting language (XBRL). One use of XBRL is for the International Financial Reporting Standard (IFRS) reporting, which is being adopted for SEC reporting; another is for Solvency II, an emerging global insurance enterprise risk management standard that originated in Europe.

An information taxonomy, or data model, uses discrete divisions or categories of data or subject areas, also called facets, to organize data and includes the specific *entities* (subject areas), *attributes* (characteristics), and relationships involved in a business function's view of information. These subject areas, or entities, are usually two to three levels deep with up to 15 terms at each level. It also provides logic for hierarchies and associations for relationships between the data such as the Party and Agreement.

There are generally at least eight major subject areas in an insurance data model which include **Account** (overall relationship with an insurer/health plan), **Party** (and role, for example, insured, member, producer, service provider, employee—adjuster, underwriter, and so on); **Policy** (or Contract); **Insurable Object** (home, car, and such); **Claim** (event); **Money or Finance** (premiums, losses, commissions, and so on), **Geography** (Risk, Loss, and such), and **Reinsurance Agreement**. Each of these subject areas is then further broken down to a second level of detail.

Life insurers would have similar data model entities (or subject areas) to those used by property and casualty companies, but would rename them (for example, Claim might be retitled as Claim/Benefit); would extend them (for example, Party would also include beneficiary); or may add entities to address life and annuity and investment specific data and transactions such as loans and withdrawals.

Health insurers would also likewise rename entities and subject areas. They would also add and extend some entities; Party would include not only members and producers, but also healthcare service providers; they would add clinical subject areas for "encounters;" and reflect additional clinically related areas such as procedures, DRGs (diagnostic related groups), and so on.

Figure 6-3 is a good example of a P&C Industry Analytics Data Model from the Object Management Group (OMG), an industry standards consortium.

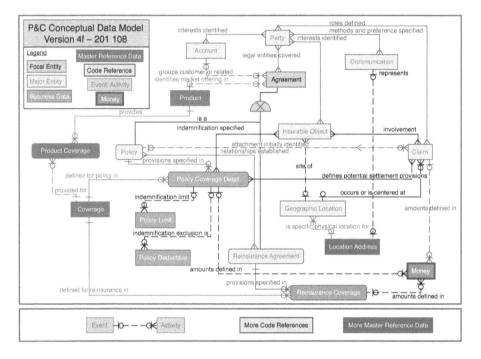

Figure 6-3 OMG P&C Conceptual Data Model

Data Model Uses

Data models are used in many ways. A major use is for data governance, data quality, and related principles such as master data management. Data models enable the data architecture and data governance teams to make data easier to find and ensure its quality and its understandability.

Data models are also extremely valuable when an organization wants to develop, redesign, or extend its data warehouse or analytics environment. Regardless of how an organization opts to physically build out its analytics environment, it still needs a way to logically organize its data assets.

A data model scope can be enterprise wide across all subject areas or by subject area like marketing, underwriting, or claims. Leading practice is to create an enterprise data model with logical views by subject area (business topic). Data models can be physical (how data is physically stored in a database) or logical (how the data is used or viewed in business relationships.)

Data models are used to store and access data in transactional as well as analytic databases. Organizations sometimes mistakenly believe that a transactional systems data model is also an analytics data model. Although an operational data model may support operational business intelligence, a separate analytics model is needed to support the full spectrum of analytics.

Many analytics applications or predefined reporting data marts include a data model; however these are not enterprise data models. These models are limited to the subject area scope of the dart mart or reports provided. The emphasis in this chapter is on enterprise data management architecture and data management: models and processes that span across all processes from an analytics perspective.

Build or Buy

Some organizations have created their own custom data models in-house; many of these had preexisting data models before the availability predefined insurance industry data models, which are now available. However, leading practice today is to purchase an insurance industry data model and adapt it to individual company needs. Even organizations that prefer building a model in-house can use predefined models as a reference data model.

Predefined models have many advantages. In-house developed data models are often created in a vacuum, which leads to higher initial development and ongoing maintenance costs and don't take advantage of industry and cross-industry collaboration. Many predefined models are mapped to industry standards organizations such as the Association for Cooperative Research & Development (ACORD), a standards organization for Property and Casualty, Life, and Reinsurance sectors.

ACORD originated developing forms and data standards for electronic data interchange (EDI) of data between key parties engaged in insurance transactions, for example, agencies and insurance companies, insurers, and reinsurers.

ACORD has evolved and now has created the **ACORD Information Framework**, which includes five facets or views of the insurance landscape designed to provide an Enterprise Reference Architecture for the insurance industry (illustrated in Figure 6-4):

- **Business glossary:** Contains common business terms with definitions (non-technical definitions) found within the insurance domain. It can be utilized to bridge communication gaps and provides context across all business areas. It contains more than 3,100 business terms.

  Value: Foundation and/or reference to develop a data dictionary to increase BI and analytics adoption.

- **Capability model:** Defines what the insurance industry does and serves as a baseline of a company's capabilities. Its scope begins with insurance companies but is not limited to insurers.

  Value: Good reference for understanding business processes and for business process mapping to improve business processes.

- **Information model:** Organizes, explains, and relates insurance concepts. It is a single model and provides a "big picture" view of the industry. This model is about concepts, not literal implementations.

  Value: Provides a common picture and language for information subject areas for joint projects involving both business and IT

- **Data model:** Generated from the Information Model to provide content alignment and traceability and also ensures the two models are always synchronized. The Data Model makes the abstract more tangible by turning concepts from Information Model into a format that can be used for persistence (for example, storage).

  Value: Helps create a physical data model for databases, providing a baseline for data warehouses, validating your data model. (Note: May be more applicable for transactional versus analytics data models.)

- **Component model:** Marries capabilities (business processes) and information; defines a design framework for the independent development of components that interoperate to form applications. Uses technology neutral interfaces for implementation across development platforms.

  Value: Identifies components that are reusable across multiple applications and interchangeable with other components.

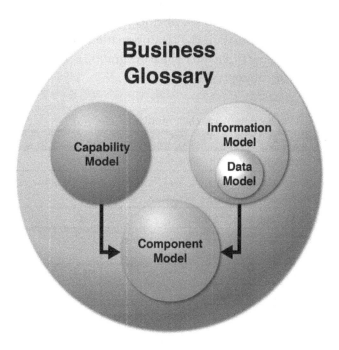

Figure 6-4 Enterprise Reference Architecture

ACORD is also a member of other standards bodies such as the Object Management Group (OMG), an association for cross industry data models and subject areas such as finance, human resources, and cross industry business processes. Note that insurers (and vendors) need to be a member to access some of the standards and assets from ACORD. ACORD has also worked with other industry professional organizations including America's Health Insurance Plans (AHIP), Life Office

Management Association (LOMA), and Reinsurance Association of America (RAA) to provide as broad an industry scope as possible. ACORD's scope is global and it has engaged in every region, providing forums and educational programs as well as participating in working groups in both mature and emerging industry markets.

Table 6-1 lists some of the most common commercially available pre-defined enterprise analytics data models available for the insurance industry. In considering the purchase of a data model, an insurance organization should check to see whether the model has been and continues to be synced with the ACORD Information Model to ensure subject area scope; doing so should reduce integration conflict and increase systems and data interoperability.

Table 6-1   Insurance Industry Data Models

Model Name	Vendor/Organization
ACORD Information Model (All Domains)	ACORD
Life Insurance, Healthcare Insurance, and Property & Casualty Data Models	ADRM Software
IIDM (Insurance Industry Data Model)	CSC
IDW (Insurance Data Warehouse), an extension of IAA (Insurance Applications Architecture)	IBM
Property-Casualty	OMG
IDF (Insurance Data Foundation)	Oracle
IWS (Information Warehouse Solution) for Property & Casualty, Life & Health Insurers	SAP Sybase
FS-DM (Financial Services-Data Model)	Teradata

Data Governance and Data Management Roles

One of the most valuable and least visible processes within an organization is data governance and data stewardship. Data governance usually has two distinct parts: governance rules and governance actions. The latter comes into play and is critical to support strategic initiatives and innovations like mergers and acquisitions, reorganizations, new product introductions, new legislation, and so on. Leading practice is to have dedicated staff in the BICC that oversees a data governance program.

The diligent efforts of data stewards help provide continuity and consistency of an organization's data. Data stewards are usually business analysts who work with specific subject area data on a regular basis and make sure that data definitions, business rules for calculations, and many other mundane but important tasks are completed. Without these efforts you would have data chaos and inconsistency.

In the property and casualty industry, many of these information professionals belong to the Insurance Data Management Association (IDMA), a professional and education organization. Even if an organization is not in the property and casualty industry sector, it can use many of the leading practices advocated by IDMA. Non-insurance professional data management organizations also exist; Data Management International (DAMA) is one of the best known. Often insurance data management professionals belong to both industry and cross-industry organizations.

Data Management Roles

Several key roles or functions are needed for data management. As mentioned previously, the key role business users fulfill is as data stewards, but data stewards work with many other roles. The following are the most common ones used in data management:

- **Information architects** are responsible for establishing the principles by which data management activities will be executed, and establishing the goals, objectives, and standards of the organization's information architecture. Area: IT and BICC

- **Data modelers** are responsible for creating, documenting, reconciling, and maintaining logical and physical models reflecting the state and use of data across the business. Area: IT

- **Database administrators** (DBAs) are responsible for the physical implementation and ongoing support of operational and business-intelligence-oriented databases. Area: IT

- **Metadata specialists** are responsible for the capture, integration, and publication of descriptive metadata across the various applications and tools (modeling, integration, and more) in the environment. Area: IT

- **Data quality specialists** are responsible for the analysis and measurement of data quality levels, identification of data quality issues, and working with data stewards, users, and other IT functions to facilitate data quality improvement. Area: IT

- **Data stewards** are responsible for the overall activity on data quality improvement, establishing of data quality goals, and effecting change in organization and business processes to achieve those goals. Area: Business

- **Data integration specialists** are responsible for the deployment and use of data integration tools to implement data acquisition, transformation, movement, and delivery. Area: IT

Data Management Tools

Special tools are often used to document and manage data. The following section highlights a few of these key tools:

- A *data dictionary* is a metadata repository, which is a centralized repository of "data about data," such relationships to other data, origin, usage, and format, that is, the *metadata*. Most data dictionaries are automated and available as specialized software with preformatted fields and interfaces for use by both business users and IT.

- *Master data management (MDM)* is a set of processes, governance, policies, standards, and tools that consistently defines and manages master data: the nontransactional data entities of an organization. Specialized MDM software is used to support master data management to remove duplicates, standardize data, conduct mass data maintenance, and incorporate business rules to eliminate incorrect data from entering the system and creating an authoritative source of *master data*.

- *Master data* are the products, accounts (policies/contracts) and parties (policyholders/members or agents/brokers/producers), with whom business is transacted. MDM is needed due to multiple business units and processes creating data redundancy. MDM provides processes for collecting, aggregating, matching, consolidating, quality-assuring, persisting, and distributing this master data throughout an organization to ensure its consistency, maintenance, and use.

Summary

Learning Objectives

Test your basic knowledge of the main points in this chapter by answering the following questions:

- Understand what enterprise information architecture is and why enterprise information architecture and data standards are critical to analytics.

- Contrast logical versus physical data models and describe the value of a logical view to the business.

- Understand key roles in data management and primary roles for business users.

- Gain a high-level overview of the data subject areas in insurance data models.

Discussion Questions

Further check your application of key concepts by reviewing the following discussion questions:

- Describe the difference between a logical and business view of data.

- Explain three causes of ineffective information architectures.

- Name and discuss three challenges in effective information architecture.

Key Terms

Data governance refers to the overall management and programmatic approach to ensure the availability, usability, integrity, and security of the data in an organization. Key elements in data governance are a Data Governance Council, data governance procedures and data stewards, and a data governance policy that specifies who is accountable for various portions or aspects of the data, including its accuracy, accessibility, consistency, completeness, and updating.

Information architecture is the structural design of shared information environments; it supports the ability to share and exchange information assets within and outside the organization. It includes a set of requirements, principles, and data models.

Logical data model (LDM) is a business representation of an organization's data, organized by entities and relationships regardless of any data management technology.

Master data management (MDM) is a technology-enabled discipline in which business and IT work together to ensure the uniformity, accuracy, stewardship, semantic consistency and accountability of the enterprise's official shared master data assets. Master data is the consistent and uniform set of identifiers and extended attributes that describes the core entities of the enterprise including customers, prospects, citizens, suppliers, sites, hierarchies, and chart of accounts. (Source: Gartner Group)

Extended Business Reporting Language (XBRL) is a language for the electronic communication of business information that provides benefits in the preparation, analysis, and communication of business information in cost-savings, greater efficiency, and improved accuracy and reliability. It is one of a family of "XML" languages that uses a standard means of communicating information between businesses and on the Internet. (Source: XBRL International)

Additional Resources/Reading

Books

Cook, Melissa A. *Building Enterprise Information Architectures*. Prentice Hall. 1996.

Silverston, Len. *Data Model Resource Book*, Vol. 1 and 2. Wiley & Sons. 2001.

Berson, Alex and Larry Duboy. *Master Data Management and Data Governance*. 2nd Ed. McGraw-Hill. 2011.

Professional Associations

ACORD (Association for Cooperative Research & Development) www.acord.org is a global nonprofit association founded in 1970 that facilitates the development and implementation of data standards and standardized forms for the insurance industry and related industries. The ACORD Framework is an insurance industry standard framework for business processes, enterprise data models, and industry metrics and KPIs. ACORD also presents events, videos, research papers, and analysis that offer insights into current industry technology and business topics. ACORD members include hundreds of insurance and reinsurance companies, agents and brokers, software providers, and associations worldwide.

IDMA (Insurance Data Management Assn.) www.idma.org is an independent, nonprofit, professional development association dedicated to increasing the level of professionalism, knowledge, and visibility of insurance data management. IDMA publishes a highly recommended data management course, Data Management for Insurance Professionals, and has co-authored content for the AIDM (Associate Insurance Data Manager) and CIDM (Certified Insurance Data Manager) professional designation curricula, certified by the Insurance Institute of America. The following text is highly recommended as an introduction to the Insurance Data Management: Insurance Data Collection and Reporting Text, 12th edition, IDMA, Jersey City, NJ, 2013.

OMG (Object Management Group) www.omg.org is an international, open membership, not-for-profit computer industry standards consortium. OMG Task Forces develop enterprise integration standards for a wide range of technologies and an even wider range of industries. OMG's modeling standards enable powerful visual design, execution and maintenance of software, and other processes.

XBRL International www.xbrl.org is a not-for-profit consortium of more than 600 companies and agencies worldwide working together to build the XBRL language and promote and support its adoption. This collaborative effort has produced a variety of specifications and taxonomies to support the goal of providing a standard, XML-based language for digitizing business reports in accordance with the rules of accounting in each country or with other reporting regimes such as banking regulation or performance benchmarking.

7

Analytics Tools

*B*I *adoption* and lack of adoption is an issue in insurance as well as other industries. Statistics from technology analyst firms estimate that only 10% of enterprise employees in any industries use business intelligence today; in insurance, use is higher but the adoption rate is still less than 20%. These same analysts project that by 2020, 75% of enterprise employees will need to use analytics, in view of the growth of data and the continued evolution of businesses becoming more data driven.

This low analytics adoption is due to a number of factors; lack of data access and data confidence are one area. Chapter 6, "Data and Information Architecture," explores how effective data and information management can improve accessibility. User skill gaps and overall analytic corporate culture is another area Chapter 9, "Analytic Skills and Culture," explores. Complexity of tools and difficulty or ease of use is yet a third; you explore the variety of BI tools available and how to choose the right tools for the right user in this chapter.

Different types of users have different needs, and these should be reflected in the tools selected and made available to them. There are an ever-increasing number of tools available from software vendors. Some are available in integrated analytics packages or suites, which combine multiple tools types; others are sold as stand-alone tools. There is a trend away from pure reporting tools, which look at historical data and "what happened," to data exploration and visualization tools, which focus on "what is happening now," and ultimately to predictive tools, which look at "what can happen" and that help identify how to drive wanted behavior. End users increasingly expect that any analysis, regardless of tool, can be shared readily and easily accessed via mobile devices—especially reports and dashboards, as shown in Figure 7-1.

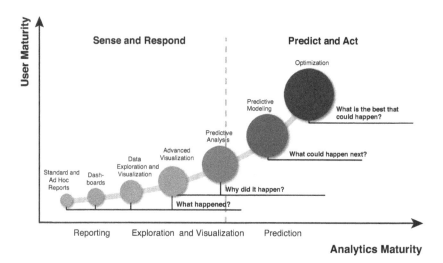

Figure 7-1 Analytic Tools Evolution

Excel as an Analytic Tool

Despite the plethora of analytic tools available, the most commonly used analytic tool is Microsoft Excel, especially in the finance area. Using Excel for analytics has certain advantages; two key ones are no additional license cost, as it is already included in an existing user license, and the familiar interface. But using Excel as a BI tool also has disadvantages, the main one is data management; often users create new "spread marts" or spreadsheet data marts, which are desktop or unofficial data sources that create further data ambiguity.

Most professional analytic tools that have an Excel "add-in" or an Excel interface capability that allow these tools to mimic Excel's usability and leverage existing user skills but also provide the data management capabilities and added functionality (advanced visualization and other functions) and administration (common data access and security rights) not included in Excel alone.

Suites Versus Stand-Alone Tools

Leading practice is to *standardize*, or consolidate, tools on an integrated analytic suite or package for lower cost, common user interface, and ease of administration. The integration refers to common data structures or semantic (logical business versus physical) views to access data and other capabilities that can be leveraged across all the tools in the suite. Another benefit of integrated suites is a common user interface for ease of usability, which leads to higher user analytic adoption, for example, common dashboard components or graphics components used in reports, dashboards, data exploration, and predictive modeling tools. Administration refers to features such as user data access rights definition; these rights are defined in a common module or facility accessed by all tools in the suite instead of having to define within each tool. Sometimes a need arises for a capability that is not included in an organization's analytics standard package; in that case IT helps identify and evaluate additional tools to meet additional requirements. However, varying from the BI standard suite should be limited to the exception based on true need.

Structured Data Analytics Tool Types

The majority of analytics tools are structured data analytics tools; these tools fall into several broad categories.

- **Dashboards:** Have a "cockpit" look and are designed to focus on high-level metrics or key performance indicators (KPIs). Are formatted into various windows (key metrics, time series window, correlation metrics, and regional/product views) and often contain "widgets" such as slider bars, dials, and so on for limited what-if analysis on predefined assumptions. Ideally, dashboards are part of a package and allow drill down into root cause analysis persisting the selected measures or attributes selected from the dashboard.

  In the Figure 7-2 dashboard for a health insurer, you see several components used to visualize data. The strategic initiatives box in the upper-left corner lists the top four initiatives and related KPIS with stop lights. Other areas on the dashboard support these initiatives with more information. The upper-right box

---

monitors losses for the top five critical diagnostic conditions. The lower-left box tracks enrollment, which is related to member growth strategic initiative. The lower-right box monitors utilization by service type or region. Speedometers track loss severity and frequency. The line of business pie chart uses radio buttons to display premiums or losses.

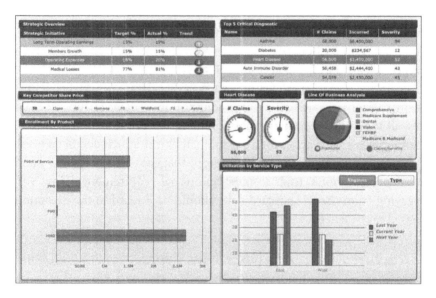

Figure 7-2 Health Insurance Executive Dashboard

■ **Data discovery and visualization:** Include easy-to-navigate interfaces for data exploration. Some tools have a Google-like text search feature to find data sets and/or parameters (measures or attributes) easily. Use a graphic interface to visualize data explored; many also include default graphics based on data selection. Most also allow merging of multiple data sets (so called mash-ups) and data manipulation (grouping, splitting, and so on), data enhancement (for example, time or geographic hierarchies), and calculations (averages, sums, and such). *Advanced visualization* tools are emerging, such as 3-D analytics.

As an example in distribution management, a marketing manager could select metrics such as Applications, Policies-in-Force, or Premiums; these metrics could further be viewed by New Business versus Renewals, Time Period, Region, Product, Customer Tenure, and so on. If you focus on a geographic attribute such as sales territory, you might want to use maps to compare regions and even drill down within a region. If you focused on product mix, you would probably use a pie chart or linen chart. Figure 7-3 shows some common graphics widely available in most data exploration and visualization tools; many are also available in dashboard and reporting tools as well. Some tools will suggest a default based on the data itself; as users grow more proficient, they can select their own preferred representations.

Sample Discovery and Visualization Options

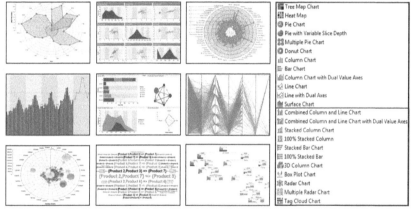

Figure 7-3 Exploration and Visualization Chart

- **Reporting:** Ad hoc and preformatted reporting tools. Some tools access flat files; others access data cubes and structures (for example, OLAP, MOLAP, and ROLAP). Ad-hoc reporting can be truly ad-hoc where expert users can create their own reports or allow customization of predefined reporting templates with key measures and attributes. Preformatted reporting is used for reports that you do not want to have altered or modified, such as regulatory reporting or management reporting.

- **Predictive:** Used to forecast and predict events. Include predictive model definition and execution; usually also include data preparation (extraction, data manipulation, and so on) capabilities and visualization of end results. Usually include a library of predefined or customer defined predictive algorithms and/or predictive models. Table 7-1 consists of frequently used algorithms by category with common applications they are used in.

Table 7-1   Predictive and Data Mining Algorithms and Applications

Functionality	Algorithm	Applicability
Classification	Logistic Regression (GLM) Decision Trees Naïve Bayes Support Vector Machine	Response modeling Recommending "next likely product" Employee retention Credit default modeling
Regression	Multiple Regression (GLM) Support Vector Machine	Credit scoring Customer profitability modeling
Anomaly detection	One Class SVM (Support Vector Machine)	Claims fraud Network intrusion
Attribute importance	Minimum Description Length (MDL)	Surgery preparation, triage Net promoter score
Association rules	Apriori	Market basket analysis
Clustering	Hierarchical K-Means Hierarchical O-Cluster	Customer segmentation Gene and protein analysis
Feature extraction	Non-Negative Matrix Factorization (NMF)	Text analysis, search

The matrix in Table 7-2 further illustrates various analytics tools including key characteristics and example uses.

Table 7-2   BI/Analytics Tool Guide Matrix

Tool Type: Purpose	Characteristics	Example Uses
Reporting: Share	Consistent layout and format; repetitive usage. Predesigned/defined content; strong distribution needs; preformatted and printable	External reporting Management
Dashboards: Engage	KPIs; time series analysis; visualize information; aggregated data structures; interactive; simple	Performance management Scorecards
Discovery and visualization: Explore and visualize	*Basic:* Highly visual; explore data for trends, outliers; highly interactive *Advanced:* Data Access; merger/combination; enrichment and manipulation	Sales management reporting
Predictive: Forecast and predict	Algorithm libraries; predefined models; data preparation, modeling/mining; result visualization	Marketing segmentation and campaign management

User Categories and Recommended Structured Data Tool Types

The most frequent categorization of users follows:

- **Executives/senior management/boards:** Monitor, analyze, and explore companywide, divisional, or regional results. Heavy users of mobile devices especially iPads or tablets.

  Key tools used: Dashboards, data exploration tools. Likely to request further analysis from others.

- **Middle management:** Monitor, analyze, and explore departmental, branch, or line of business results; a level below executive/senior management/boards. Share information with executives or senior management; likely to incorporate into briefing book presentations. Desktop or mobile device users.

Key tools used: Dashboards, reports, data discovery, and visualization.

- **Business analysts:** Analyze results proactively or in response to requests from management. Create, edit, and share analysis. Often prefer Excel-like interfaces, especially financial analysts. Desktop and mobile users.

Key tools used: Ad hoc reporting tools, advanced data discovery and visualization, predictive analysis.

- **Data scientists/predictive analysts:** Prepare data, create and run algorithms, and share findings for further use. Need advanced data access, calculation and manipulation capabilities. Desktop and cloud users.

Key tools used: Predictive analytics, text analysis, event detection, and data visualization.

User Maturity and Tool Evaluation Tip

Analytic sand boxes, dedicated test environments, are often used to encourage use of new tools or provide an evaluation environment to provide feedback on tools being evaluated. These environments help increase user adoption by providing a collaborative user and IT lab. BI Competency Centers often create and manage sand boxes from a governance perspective, for example, define its purpose, determine who has access, identify and license tools, gather evaluation feedback, and so on.

Unstructured Data Analytics Tools and Text Mining

Most of the tools discussed previously have focused on structured data. Increasingly, text and other unstructured data types (photographs, diagrams, and so on) are being "mined" for insights using text mining. Text mining ranges from the simplest Boolean searches used in Google and other search engines to more sophisticated *sentiment analysis* (also called *opinion mining*), which evaluates feelings (for example, attitudes, emotions, opinions, and such) as positive, negative, or neutral.

Text mining, also referred to as *text data mining* or *text analytics,* derives insight from text. Text mining structures text using parsing and other techniques such as *Natural Language Processing (NLP).* Text taxonomies and vocabularies are also used to categorize data and to define synonyms, as well as define certain "stop" words that can result in "false" search results.

Typical text mining analytics tasks include text categorization, text clustering, concept/entity extraction (automatic tagging), text taxonomies, document summarization, and entity relationship modeling (that is, relations between entities). Text mining is also used in *Enterprise Content Management,* a discipline within the broader data management and information architecture arena.

Text analysis involves information retrieval, lexical analysis to study word frequency distributions, pattern recognition, tagging/annotation, information extraction, and data mining techniques including link and association analysis, visualization (for example, tag clouds) and predictive analytics. In the tag cloud the size of the typeface usually represents the number of "hits" or frequency with which a word or term has been used in a document in the subject analysis.

A typical application is to scan a set of documents and model the document set for classification or to populate a database or search index with the information extracted.

Typical applications in insurance are for customer and producer sentiment, claims or underwriting application fraud detection, claims subrogation analysis, emerging loss exposure analysis, and more. Text analysis can be used to identify additional coded values needed for structured data (toxic mold as a code for the cause of loss field) or even the need for additional structured data fields.

Platforms

BI tools can be installed on mobile devices, on the desktop, on shared servers, in the "cloud" and on mainframes. There is a major movement to cloud-based software. Business users need not be concerned with where BI tools are installed as long as they are available to them when and where they need them.

BI Tool Costs and BI Standardization

License costs are only one element of the total cost of ownership (TCO) for BI costs. BI costs can be grouped into five major cost categories: BI software licensing, BI software licensing maintenance, administration, help/support desk, and user training.

You should care as a business person for two reasons: 1) ease of use/usability—having a common interface for as many of your tools as practical makes it easier for you to use them; and 2) cost—ultimately the business pays for BI tools and related costs.

Table 7-3 provides more detail on these costs and average cost guidelines per area.

Table 7-3 BI Total Cost of Ownership Components

Cost Category	Description	Guidelines
BI Software License Costs	Software Licensing Costs	Licensing models vary; trend toward Concurrent Session Based Licenses vs. Named User Licenses
BI Software License Maintenance Costs (20% of software license)	Annual Software Maintenance Costs	Traditionally 20% of software License costs per year
Administration Costs (100K + 40% benefits load factor)	BI Administrative Staff (annual salary + benefits loading)	X staff per XX BI Users
BI Help Desk/Support Costs (Avg. Cost Per Call - $20)	BI Help Desk/Support Staff	3 calls per day per BI User
User Training Costs (Avg. Cost Per Course — $1,500)	User Training Costs	25% of BI users take one course per year

According to the Gartner Group, a technology analyst firm, "Companies resisting the need to consolidate BI tools will incur 50% more cost for each redundant tool." With such a significant cost-savings, more organizations are trying to rationalize the multiple BI tools they own and standardize on a single BI suite.

Summary

Learning Objectives

Test your basic knowledge of the main points in this chapter by answering the following questions:

- Compare major tool types, what they do, and how they can be used.

- Contrast typical user classification categories, information needs, and appropriate tools.

- Understand benefits of BI Consolidation.

Discussion Questions

Further check your application of key concepts by reviewing the following discussion questions:

- Explain two advantages and disadvantages of using Excel as a BI tool.

- Describe two advantages of using a BI suite/package versus stand-alone BI tools.

- Compare three cost-savings areas through BI standardization.

Key Terms

Analytic sand box: An environment in which users and developers can "play" with tools, data sets, and so on.

Ad hoc reports: A one-off report or customization of a standard report. Standard reports are reports that are regularly produced and/or viewed.

BI standardization: A process to reduce or rationalize the number of software applications. The ultimate intent is to select a standard BI vendor and default to its products unless there is a need not met by the portfolio of products. Benefits are lower total cost of ownership and broader user adoption from a common platform and interface.

(BI) Dashboard: A dashboard is a data visualization tool that provides metrics and Key Performance Indicators (KPIs) on a single screen, much like the dashboard on your car. They can be designed for a specific role or designed from a summary to detail by "view" within a function. Often include widgets like speedometers, sliders, and so on. Should include the ability to drill through to further detail in reports or ad hoc analysis persisting or carrying forward data selection criteria from the initial dashboard view. Also see (Balanced) Scorecard.

Data discovery: The act or process of discovering insights in data.

Scorecard (Balanced Score Card — BSC): See Chapter 4, "Defining and Using Metrics Effectively."

Visualization: Visual representation of business intelligence or analysis using a variety of graphic representations such as pie charts, bar charts, heat maps, tag clouds, and so on.

Additional Resources/Reading:

Books

Spangler, Scott and Jeffrey Kreulen. *Mining the Talk: Unlocking the Business Value in Unstructured Information.* IBM Press/Pearson, plc. 2008.

Eckerson, Wayne. *Performance Dashboards: Measuring, Monitoring & Managing Your Business.* John Wiley & Sons. 2010.

Siegel, Eric and Thomas H. Davenport. *Predictive Analytics: The Power to Predict Who Will Click, Buy, Lie, or Die.* John Wiley & Sons. 2013.

Tufte, Edward. *The Visual Display of Quantitative Information.* Graphics Press. 2001. A classic reference work; the original "bible" of visualization. Tools may change, but good design principals remain constant. Two noteworthy related books by the same author are *Envisioning Information* (1990) and *Visual Explanations* (1997).

8

Organization and Implementation

nalytics continue to evolve as business needs change and as new capabilities become available. A BI or analytic strategy also needs to adapt. Processes, people, and technologies are all required to maintain and update the strategy. A *BI Competency Center (BICC)*, sometimes also called a BI Center of Excellence (CoE), is key to addressing all three of these areas.

BICCs have been around for several years and continue to exist for good reason; they are effective in governing priorities, sharing best practices, managing costs, selecting tools, driving analytic adoption, and advocating analytic culture development. Organizations with a BICC deliver higher levels of insight, make better use of information assets, deliver reduced costs, have better data quality, and are more agile than those without. According to the technology research firm Gartner Group, organizations with a BICC require 2.8 full-time IT resources to support 100 active users versus 4.0 resources for those without a BICC. BICCs also attain additional savings in development time and software licensing costs. Many organizations are also developing BI Communities of Practice (CoPs) to share best practices and facilitate peer mentoring. Although these communities are quite valuable, they only complement but are not a substitute for a BICC.

Figure 8-1 shows the major key areas that fall under the BICC: Overall Governance Structure or Organization; Program Governance; Defining the BI Roadmap and Milestones; BI KPIs and Measurement, Training, and Education; and End User Support. Business users interact with BICCs in a number of ways within the organization's overall BI strategy including defining business needs and business value, finding the

BI program, participating in data governance, training and education, and support. The following sections review these various areas in more detail.

Figure 8-1 BI Strategy Framework

Objectives and Scope

First and foremost the BICC is responsible for defining, documenting, and communicating the organization's BI strategy objectives and scope including the background and purpose, current state and history, and current and future objectives and scope. The BICC leader works with various committees in the organization and governance to ensure that the BI strategy is business driven and aligned with the overall organization's business strategy. Business users participate in business requirements definition, prioritization, funding, and data stewardship through the governance structure.

Organization and Governance Structure

BICCs govern through committees. Typically organizations create levels of committees and appoint committee members: Level 1 - Executive Steering Committees; Level 2 - Operating or Working Steering Committees, and Level 3 - Individual Contributors and IT Delivery Organization. Executives and senior managers participate in executive and operating committees, who work with IT and with individual contributors from the business areas to prioritize BI project requests and allocate funding for the overall program.

Other key areas that are part of the organization and governance structure are end user training and education, and ongoing support. Employee onboarding, including familiarization with organizational tools and standard reports, is critical to support a decision-driven culture. Ongoing support in the use of BI tools and with any data access or system performance issues is also needed. Many organizations have added communities of practice and/or internal user groups for self-help and mentoring. They are also adding online user communities to share new reports, capabilities, new sources available, and so on. Many have also the role of communication analyst to manage these new sites and capabilities.

A *Self Service BI* strategy and capabilities have become paramount. As organizations increase their analytic maturity and demand for analytics, it is impossible for IT to fulfill user requests on a timely basis. Further, increasingly sophisticated end users want to create their own reports and visualizations. IT's role has become one of data provisioning, creating easier access to data, maintaining infrastructure, and providing appropriate BI tools.

For self-service BI to be successful, four key areas must be addressed (as shown in Figure 8-2):

- **Governance:** Addresses what the self-service scope is by user role and ensures that the existing governance structure has been updated to support self-service roles and capabilities.

- **Adoption:** Identifies needs to support a self-service analytic culture and the end user training needed. For example, this may include developing a community of interest/practice or mentors.

- **Data:** Defines data access rights, ensures that data is understandable (definition, calculations, source, and last update) by end users and that data quality is acceptable so that the user is confident in using it.

- **Technologies:** Ensures that users have the right tools for the right analyses, that an integrated platform is in place for analytic reuse and sharing, and that a semantic layer with business views exists to provide ease of access to the data.

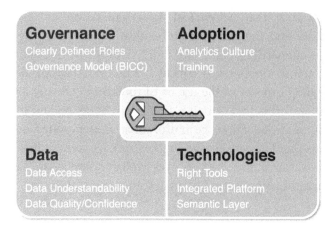

Figure 8-2 Keys to Self-Service BI Success

Business Needs

Business areas should review, reprioritize, and update BI needs annually as part of the annual planning process and submit requests for projects and capabilities needed to support their key initiatives for the next 12 to 18 months. Tactically, various ad hoc requests will also arise during the year.

The BICC should have a standardized request process and a request review committee, usually as part of the overall strategic and/or working committees. The business usually has assigned individuals to business analyst and data steward roles as part of the BICC structure; these roles are often part time.

Value Measurement and Management

To prioritize requests, the projected business value for a request must be estimated. Business analysts assigned from business areas will usually define or document the value. An additional role of the KPI analyst may also be used in some organizations; this function may be filled by the business analyst or by a cost accounting analyst from finance.

Post-implementation is also important to document the actual value attained from significant projects. These value management activities contribute to value delivered by BICC and BI programs and help to ensure ongoing funding. See Chapter 5, "Analytics Value and Return on Investment," for details on an overall value-based management approach to BI Programs.

Information Structure and Technologies

Data stewards are assigned from the business area to participate in the data governance committee. They typically define data definitions including metrics and key performance indicators as well as confirm attribute values or code descriptions (for example, profit center, product type, and so on).

Data stewards are also engaged in defining the data taxonomy or logical data model definition and maintenance, and increasingly as more nonstructured data and text grows, in defining text taxonomies. Again these roles are usually filled by business analysts. IT's job is to make sure that the information architecture is effective to support the physical organization and the logical organization of the data and accessibility, as well as security.

Leading practice is use of a standard BI suite both for the lowest cost of ownership and for maximum business usability. As part of the previously mentioned self-service BI movement and advanced analysis (for example, data and text mining) needs, the BICC's role is to evaluate, select, and train users on existing and new tools. The BICC will also participate in selecting BI or analytic applications such as budgeting and planning, cost accounting, and so on.

Related Topics

BICC Program Governance

Program governance refers to the people, policies, and processes for the overall BI program. This includes the project request process, request review, and prioritization. Often IT organizations focus tactically at the project level. Program governance means looking at IT delivery programmatically or more strategically, instead of on a request by request basis. Users participate both as requestors and on committees that prioritize requests.

BI Roadmap and Milestones

Every organization should have a BI roadmap that shows major initiatives and dependencies to communicate the current and future status of the overall BI strategy. Some projects that are infrastructure or foundational are largely invisible to business users. The roadmap should be available to business users. It is usually posted on a BI community of interest forum or intranet site.

BICC KPIs and Measurement

BICCs need to communicate measureable results from the organization's BI program, both strategically and tactically. Key goals, objectives, KPIs, and related initiatives should be defined. One way to do so is through a BICC scorecard. Figure 8-3 shows that the BICC has four strategic themes with supporting goals and objectives. Each of these is supported by measurements and targets, as well as initiatives and associated budgets.

For example, within the Internal Customers Strategy, there are two key goals: Increasing End User Productivity and Providing Cost Effective and Innovative BI. A self-service target of 75% of all BI users has been established, which is supported with a BI upgrade project and appropriate funding. The monitoring of this and the other objectives and key metrics would be built into a BICC scorecard.

Strategy Map		Balanced Scorecard		Action Plan	
Theme: Data Driven Decisioning	**Objective**	**Measurement**	**Target**	**Initiative**	**Budget**
Financial — Lower BI TCO, Standardize BI Tools, Reduce License Fees	• Reduce BI Infrastructure Costs • Reduce BI Resource Labor Costs	• # of BI environments • Annual BI Tool maintenance and support costs	• One • < $75k	• BI Tool Consolidation Project • Co-term SW License Negotiations	• $150k • 1 FTE (80 hrs.)
Internal Customers — Increase End User Productivity, Provide Cost-Effective and innovative BI	• Provide efficient and easier access to info • Provide latest BI SW capabilities	• End-User Satisfaction Survey • # of Self-Service Users • # of BI Services available	• 85% Favorable • 75% • 15 Services	• Online User Survey Project • BI Upgrade	• $5k • $350k
IT Service Management — Increase efficiency, Training, Support	• Improve 1st time incident resolution • Develop Online Training Programs • Improve tracking of BI support incidents	• % of 1st time incident resolutions • Time to resolve BI incidents • # of online BI training courses	• 60% • 4 hours • 10 intro, 5 advanced	• BI-specific Education Program • BI Incident Management improvement Program • Service Desk Reengineering Program	• $150k • $150k • $200k
Learning — Knowledge Management Repository, BI Sandbox	• Develop necessary BI skills • Develop BI Sandbox for innovation	• # of repository entries • Avg. rating of entry • Availability of BI Sandbox	• 50 per month • 4 out of 5 • 95.999%	• Repository incentive program • Configure BI Sandbox	• $50k • $100k

Source: SAP BusinessObjects 2009 Australia Insight Conference Presentation

BI Competency Centers: People + Information = Intelligence

Figure 8-3 BICC Strategy Map and Scorecard Example

Figure 8-4 shows sample tactical metrics for BICC Return Delivered and Operations Performance, which could be included in a BICC dashboard or scorecard. Return Delivered includes projects, costs, usage, and quality. Operations Performance includes system and data availability, load time, outages, and training.

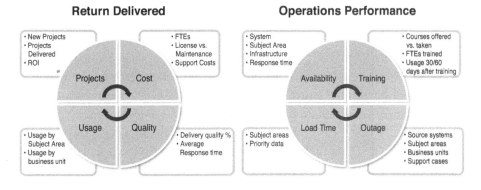

Figure 8-4 BICC Metrics

Training and Education

User training and education includes defining training curricula by role, identifying emerging training and education needs, evaluating training program effectiveness including its impact on user analytic adoption, and user support. Courses in the use of specific products are provided by software vendors. Organizations can license courses on broader conceptual topics and make them available via their knowledge management intranets. Many trade and professional associations also provide courses as part of certifications or continuing education programs. Technology analyst firms and specialty technical and analytic organizations provide dedicated analytics conferences or forums.

With the increased demand for analytics and self-service, there is a strong demand for training in visualization techniques, data mining, text mining, geographic information systems, integrating social media, and third-party data. The curricula need to be continually updated to include new technologies, tools, and concepts. Business users must make their needs known so that HR, training, and BICCs can review and update their course catalogs.

BICCs should also work with HR on analytic skills aptitude as part of broader human capital and talent analytics management programs. This evaluation measures aptitude by analytic role and is useful not only in new employee hiring but also in determining where to invest training and development resources and in career development, based on overall potential analytic aptitude. See Chapter 9, "Analytics Skills and Culture," for more detail on skills.

User Support

Whether business users use IT developed reports or create their own, they will encounter issues that could be related to system response, security, data availability, or other areas. Business users can get support from the IT help desk and the BICC. Typically, the first-level response is provided by IT, with the second-level response provided by the BICC. Analysis of support requests can provide valuable feedback for training and education programs and future BI capabilities needed.

BICC Organization Structures

BICCs can take many forms; these are dependent on an organization's culture and state of its BI maturity. There is no right or wrong form; each has advantages and disadvantages. Table 8-1 shows four common forms along with pros and cons.

Table 8-1   BICC Organization Forms

Form	Advantage	Disadvantage
BICC as Part of IT (a department with IT)	■ BI initiatives can be centrally coordinated within IT. ■ Simpler to manage due to clear reporting structure. ■ CIO facilitates trade-offs and alignment with other strategic initiatives.	■ Possible insufficient business input and/or business sponsorship. ■ May be viewed as pure IT imitative. ■ Long-term funding risk. ■ Lack of enterprise visibility.
Virtual BICC	■ Business input without dedicated full time resources. ■ Enterprise wide perspective and visibility.	■ Strong BICC leader and clear, matrixes roles are needed. ■ BICC performance metrics to validate responsibilities are critical. ■ Potential lack of support if virtual resources are not actually dedicated.
BICC as part of operations (or other key CXO function, for example, finance)	■ Focus on BI for business use. ■ Senior management support (COO). ■ COO facilitates trade-offs and alignment with other strategic initiatives.	■ Business and IT roles need close management. ■ May be viewed as top-down corporate mandate versus business unit-driven.

Form	Advantage	Disadvantage
Distributed BICC	■ Corporate linkage ensures full senior management support. ■ Enterprisewide perspectives and broad visibility.	■ Strong BICC leader with senior management access and participation needed. ■ Both IT and business involvement needed. ■ BICC performance metrics communication critical. ■ Business units may try to advance own individual initiatives.

The important thing is to make sure you have a BICC. If you do not have one, you can set one up starting as a pilot within 4 to 8 weeks, working with a single BI project, and add capabilities to it going forward with other BI projects.

BICC Roles and Responsibilities

Many BICC roles will be part time and some may reside in the business. But a few roles are critical; they should be full time and should reside in a dedicated BICC function, regardless of where the BICC reports. Following is a list of key roles with the role description, level of importance, and time required.

- **BICC leader:** Promotes value and potential of BI in the organization. Is responsible for ensuring that BI strategy and BI projects are aligned with corporate strategy and that they meet business requirements. Liaison between IT and the business. Establishes and monitors KPIs for BI strategy success and for the work of the BICC. Manages the BICC, vendor relations and licensing, and sponsors internal user groups. Manages BI standards and templates. Negotiates service-level agreements between BICC and the business units. Works with chief strategy officer. Resides in BICC. (Critical; full time)

- **Chief strategy officer (CSO):** Responsible for organizational analytic vision and ensures driving decisions based on information. Senior business management role. Works with BICC leader and CIO. May also be called a chief data officer (CDO); however, emphasis is on use of data versus data security and privacy. Most often a C-level position within the senior management team. (Optional; full time)

- **Business analyst:** Understands business rules and processes of the current organization. Documents the business requirements and how data is currently used in the organization and transformations or business rules that are applied to data. Can reside in BICC or in business units. (Critical; part time)

- **Chief data steward:** Identifies issues and recommends initiatives to address data quality and data integrity. Manages cross-departmental initiatives to address data issues. Develops and implements data management strategy that ensures the delivery of information. Coordinates, guides, and often chairs the data stewardship committee. Often resides in or comes from finance or actuarial due to data quality criticality in external data reporting for these areas. Resides in BICC. (Critical; part time)

- **Data steward:** Responsible for the overall activity on data quality improvement, establishing of data quality goals, and affecting change in organization and business processes to achieve those goals. Role is often filled by a business analyst residing in the business unit. Function may be performed by a business analyst residing in the business. (Critical; part time)

- **KPI analyst:** Responsible for defining Key Performance Indicators (KPIs) including the business rules for calculation and applied business value of the KPIs. This role may be played by a business analyst or by a cost accountant residing in the business. (Optional; part time)

- **Communication analyst:** Responsible for creating and maintaining the end user community and relevant content on it including the BICC scorecard or dashboard, key project successes, new training programs, key BICC contacts, governance committee meetings, data governance updates, and so on. (Optional, but increasingly important; part time)

Establishing a BICC

The BICC covers many areas that may seem overwhelming, but if you are just establishing one, you do not need to address all areas at one time. Many organizations start by developing a virtual BICC leveraging a few people within IT and engaging business users for other functions such as data stewardship business case development, and such. Often business analysts who sit in the business units become virtual BICC members.

To get the BICC started, it is critical to assign a full-time BICC Leader, select a BICC model, secure executive sponsorship, establish your overall BI Program Governance Model, define BICC metrics, and begin to make the BICC results visible throughout the organization.

Even if an organization does not have a formal BICC, most likely many of its functions exist to some degree. A capabilities review to determine the existence and degree of implementation of key BICC capabilities is highly recommended to evaluate current capabilities and gaps and to plan a roadmap for the establishment of a BICC.

Many organizations have set up a BICC with a BICC pilot. They validated and enhanced existing capabilities during the course of a selected BI project and then continued to build out additional BICC capabilities as additional BI projects were implemented.

In summary, organizations with BICCs minimize risks and maximize the value of their BI initiatives. As BICCs mature, organizations can move from a tactical to a strategic approach to a BI. Strategic investments increase as a percentage of the BI total spent rather than on tactical efforts. This strategic programmatic approach to BI and analytics projects drops to the bottom line as it helps the business deliver on strategic corporate initiatives for improved financial business performance.

Summary

Learning Objectives

Test your basic knowledge of the main points in this chapter by answering the following questions:

- Understand the role of a BICC and how business users interact with one.

- Review the trend toward a self-service BI and key elements of a self-service BI strategy.

Discussion Questions

Further check your application of key concepts by reviewing the following discussion questions:

- Review four key functions of a BICC.

- Describe three key roles in a BICC.

- Name four BICC organizational or operating model types, and give one advantage and disadvantage for each.

- Explain the two benefits that a BICC delivers.

Key Terms

BI Competency Center (BICC): The organization that champions, develops, and manages the enterprise BI strategy plan and priorities; includes related functions such as business requirements, data quality, data governance, and overall BI program governance. Sometimes called a BI Center of Excellence (CoE).

BI program governance: The strategic guiding principles, decision-making processes, and oversight procedures that support an organization's business intelligence and analytic capabilities.

(BI) self-service: The ability of end business users to create their own business intelligence reports and/or analytics with IT supported tools and architecture; moving toward more data exploration and analysis than reporting. May also include predictive analytics, data mining, and text mining.

Additional Resources/Reading

Business Intelligence and Performance Management; Key Initiative Overview. Gartner Group. 2013. (Research Brief).

Miller, Gloria J., Stephanie V. Gerlach, and Dagmar Brautigam. *Business Intelligence Competency Centers: A Team Approach to Maximizing Competitive Advantage.* John A. Wiley & Sons. 2006.

9

Analytics Skills and Culture

Data is one of the key assets of any insurance organization. But BI strategy execution and evolving the organization's analytic maturity involves not only the strategy, but it also must have people who can execute it. Not everyone needs to be a *data scientist* or even have a title that includes analyst, but everyone should be curious about and engaged in the data that they use.

Technology analyst firms project that 75% of enterprise employees will need to use analytics in their jobs by 2020; yet surveys show that only approximately 10% of employees use them today. Hiring people with basic analytic skills and analytic aptitude, as well as increasing the analytic skills and adoption for existing employees, are paramount to enabling them.

Certainly executive leadership and including analytics within the corporate vision or strategic goals sets the tone. However, the following areas must also be addressed: accountability, business alignment, communication, organization, roles and responsibilities, skills, and teamwork. This chapter addresses the skills and aptitudes needed by the business and also by IT to support the business, as well as strategies and tactics to improve employee skills and analytic aptitude as part of creating an analytic and data-driven decisioning culture.

Analytic Skills and Analytics Value Chain

To create an analytic culture and evolve analytic skills, the following must be done:

- Identify core analytical skills required.

- Explore challenges in collecting, evaluating, and presenting information.

- Communicate and embed the analytics within business processes.

Analytical skills are the ability to visualize, articulate, and make decisions that are logical and based on available information. These skills involve the ability to apply logical thinking and analytic techniques in gathering and analyzing information, designing and testing solutions to problems, and formulating plans. Skills needed vary by role; for example, not every employee needs the same skills as a data scientist or data modeler. But every employee should have a basic analytic mindset that includes understanding how analytics support the corporate mission statement and strategy and the business unit objectives, and having basic analytics skills relative to their role.

Analytic skills include

- **Data preparation:** Gathering and preparing data for analysis used later in the analytics workflow

- **Data exploration:** Viewing and analyzing data in different ways; exploring metrics or KPIs (counts, amounts, and so on) by various dimensions (geography, product, business unit, and such) over various points in time

- **Data visualization:** Analyzing data using the most relevant graphic representation, for example, pie charts, bar charts, bubble charts, geographic maps, and heat maps

- **Data extraction:** Creating a subset of data from a larger data set or combination of data sets for analysis

- **Report creation:** Creating new reports or modifying existing reports using reporting tools

- **Segmentation:** Analyzing and creating clusters or grouping of data with common characteristics (for example, income, age, and average spend), often using predictive tools

- **System development and administration:** Creating and productionalizing reusable and often automated scheduled analytics, and granting appropriate access rights to those analytics

- **Business expertise:** Possessing "domain" or business knowledge such as cross-industry business process or function, for example, finance or marketing or industry-specific such as actuarial, claims, and underwriting

- **Decisioning:** Making decisions based on data and analytics

Figure 9-1 reviews the analytic value chain and roles, and key skills and tasks needed by role.

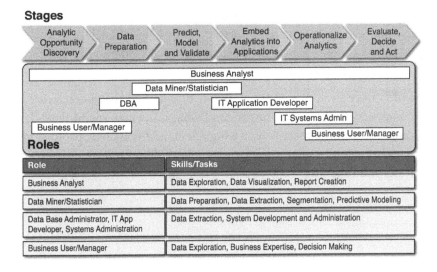

Figure 9-1 Analytic Value Chain and Users

Analytical skills are complemented by other related skills, which also vary for the business, system, or technical user. Business analysts benefit from *design thinking*, an empathetic approach used in innovation often applied for product development, business plan, problem identification, business case development, and use case development. Systems analysts or technical staff use *systems thinking*, a structured approach applied to the systems development life cycle, organizational knowledge, problem identification, and problem analyzing and solving. Collaboration between business and IT is needed for analytics and capabilities that both meet business needs and are technically sustainable.

Analytic Talent Management

Talent management refers to the planning and management of human capital including recruitment, retention, development, and performance management. McKinsey & Co. popularized and led the field through its research and publications in the early 2000s. Organizations are extending and applying this approach and including analytics aptitude testing during initial recruitment and ongoing professional development. When hiring analytics professionals (for example, data miners, statisticians, and data scientists) whose key role is analysis, this analytic aptitude evaluation should be included as part of the candidate interview and evaluation process. Further, some level of analytic aptitude evaluation should also be done when hiring any employee whose job description includes analysis.

Models have been developed to better understand the characteristics of analytics professionals, understand what tasks they spend their day doing, and because there is such a high demand for analytic professionals, to better understand what employers can do to improve attracting, hiring, and retaining them, as shown in Figure 9-2.

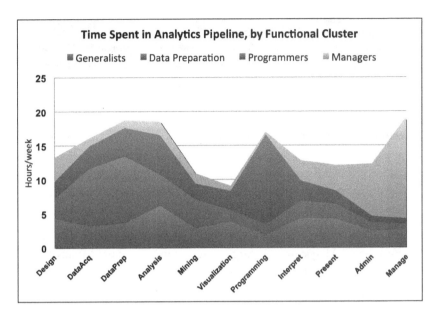

Figure 9-2 Time Allocation by Role. Source: Talent Analytics, Corp.

Culture and Adoption

It's not enough to just hire people with analytic skills, provide analytic skills as part of personal development, or to include being a data-driven company as part of the corporate mission statement. An organization cannot just "talk the talk;" it also must "walk the walk." It must reinforce the use of analytics in employees' daily jobs and in its overall culture and corporate behavior, both internally and externally. The most effective way to create an analytics culture and drive adoption is by executive and management leadership. The following case study and advertising campaign example illustrates how organizations can drive an analytic culture.

A Fortune 1000 software company wanted to improve the timeliness and accuracy of its sales forecast, which was largely done in Excel. This manual process was inconsistent resulting in an official forecast and an unofficial "shadow forecast;" this dual forecast was not only inconsistent and time consuming but also resulted in a lack of confidence in the final forecast. This put corporate management in the position of either overestimating or underestimating its sales projections, which created uncertainty and risk as it could affect its stock price.

The CEO mandated daily sales forecast updates to its official system of record, its CRM system. The organization also distributed iPads to its entire sales force and sales management team as part of its daily forecast reviews. Sales leadership changed its business processes requiring daily sales forecast updates and added both incentives and penalties for lack of "sales hygiene" to sales reps' and managers' MBOs. Today, the entire sales organization has only one forecast, and everyone has access to the numbers all the way from the sales rep to the team manager to the branch/regional manager and ultimately up to senior sales management and the board. The sales force and managers can still continue to use spreadsheets for their "personal" sales management, but everyone understands that the official numbers are in the CRM system.

Reinforcing this culture shift, the CEO went "public" touting the benefits of this shift in discussions with market analysts. As a result, sales forecasts are more accurate and management has insight that enables it to make decisions about actions that can help it meet the forecasts such as additional staffing, customer promotions, and sales incentives—decisions that are all driven by the official data from its CRM system.

CASE STUDY: UNITEDHEALTH GROUP'S "NUMBERS" ADVERTISING CAMPAIGN

UnitedHealth Group is an example of an organization with a strong analytics culture. UHG has always had strong analytic capabilities as a health insurer. UHG even created a separate subsidiary focused on providing analytics as a profit center.

It's current "Numbers" advertising campaign speaks volumes about its commitment to analytics and being data driven. The campaign uses a number of themes including "Comfort in Numbers. Support in Numbers. Simplicity in Numbers. Knowledge in Numbers. Health in Numbers."

Changing culture is difficult. Volumes have been written about "change management" and its challenges. But education and mentoring can both play a strong role in changing culture and increasing adoption.

Educational programs can help employees develop and improve their analytic skills. Some "hard," tangible skills such as learning specific software tools are available from your BI or analytic tool vendor. Broader nontool-specific courses, such as statistics or data modeling, can be recommended by corporate training and development departments or BI Competency Centers. The BICC can create a curriculum of both tool and nontool courses as part of its mandate.

Managers can foster an analytic culture by supporting employees' education and professional development, by making sure that analytics are included in MBOs and performance reviews. Managers should also reinforce application of these skills and ask for "fact-based" opinions and decisions. They can provide opportunities in on-the-job training by assigning employees as "business analysts" or domain experts on projects. They can also leverage employees with stronger skills to mentor employees who need development. Lastly, they should recommend or support employee participation in user groups and professional organizations. All these tactics can lead to improved analytic skills, analytic application, and ultimately in increased adoption.

An analytics culture supported by strong analytic skills is necessary for innovation and transformation and to provide the maximum return on investment on your people, data, and technology assets. The organization must make decisions based on analytics. Key factors in becoming a truly analytic-driven organization include executive leadership, overcoming cultural and political barriers, creating an analytic culture, and nurturing talent development. According to a Bain & Company study, organizations that were the most effective at decision making and execution delivered average shareholder returns 6% higher than other firms.

Summary

Learning Objectives

Test your basic knowledge of the main points in this chapter by answering the following questions:

- Understand key analytics skills.
- Review the Analytics Value Chain and key analytics roles across it.

Discussion Questions

Further check your application of key concepts by reviewing the following discussion questions:

- Name and explain four key analytic skills.
- Describe the role of executive leadership and managers in fostering an analytics culture.
- Discuss how education and mentoring enable change management and analytics adoption.
- Compare and contrast "design thinking" with "systems thinking."

Key Terms

Data scientists refer to quantitative analysts including statisticians, actuaries, biostatisticians, and other similar analytic roles who use advanced analytics.

Design thinking is an empathetic approach used in innovation often applied for product development, business plan, problem identification, business case development, and use case development.

Systems thinking is a structured approach applied to a systems development life cycle, organizational knowledge, problem identification, and problem analyzing and solving.

Talent management refers to the planning and management of human capital including recruitment, retention, development, and performance management.

Additional Resources/Reading

Books/Other Reading

Davenport, Thomas H., Jeanne G. Harris, and Robert Morison. *Analytics at Work: Smarter Decisions, Better Results.* Harvard Business School Publishing. 2010.

"Benchmarking Analytic Talent." Talent Analytics Corp. December 2012. (A research study on analytics professionals.)

Siegel, Eric. *Predictive Analytics: Power to Predictive Who Will Click, Buy, Lie, or Die.* John Wiley & Sons, Inc. 2013.

Michaels, Ed, Helen Handfield-Jones, and Beth Axelrod. *War for Talent.* McKinsey & Co. McKinsey & Co., Inc. 2001.

Meiser, Jeanne C. and Karie Willyerd. *The 2020 Workplace: How Innovative Companies Attract, Develop, and Keep Tomorrow's Employees Today.* Harper Collins. 2010.

Professional Associations

INFORMS (Institute for Operations Research & Management Sciences) www.informs.org. Professional organization for cross industry operations research and management professionals. Sponsors the CAP (Certified Analytic Professional) professional designation.

SIR (Society of Insurance Research) www.sirnet.org. Professional organization for insurance marketing, market research, and product development professionals.

Casualty Actuarial Society (CAS) www.casact.org. Professional association for property and casualty actuaries and actuarial candidates. Practice areas including enterprise risk management, ratemaking, predictive modeling, and reserving.

Society of Actuaries (SOA) www.soa.org. Professional association for life and health actuaries and actuarial candidates. Has created a competency framework and self-assessment test for professional development that synthesizes skills, knowledge, behaviors, attitudes, and attributes.

10

Use Cases and Case Studies

nalytics run the full value chain of insurance from product development to marketing and distribution—through underwriting, policy, and claims management—and ultimately in overall business performance management. Certainly each industry sector has its nuances but also commonalities. Some general terms are used across industry segments for business processes or analytic use cases; others are more specific by segment, for example, member is used instead of customer by health insurers or mutual insurers. Each industry segment also has unique business processes. However, many of the core business processes and analytics are fundamentally similar. Insurance industry analytics continue to evolve in many ways including moving from reactive to proactive, in the level of granularity of the data used for analysis, and in leveraging external data to augment or act as proxies for internal data, to name a few.

This chapter reviews the most common use cases across industry business process flows (or value chain) to help insurers compare their use of analytics and to stimulate ideas for additional application within their organizations.

This chapter is organized into sections: Property & Casualty (P&C), Life, and Health insurance. These sectors share many of the same common fundamental business processes such as Product, Marketing, Distribution, Underwriting, Claim, and Financial Management. Each section includes an overview of the business process and highlights key analytics used in each process with selected use cases and case studies. Use cases common to all three sectors are included in the "P&C" section; additional processes and use cases for Health or Life are listed within those sections. The term "use cases" is used as a description of an application of analytics within a business process area. Each section also includes case studies to make the use case more relevant.

Property and Casualty

The core value chain (or business processes) for property and casualty insurance include Product Management, Marketing, Distribution Management, Underwriting Management, Policy Administration and Service, Claim Management, and Financial Management. Each of these business processes requires both front-end operational analytics and reporting, typically embedded into the core processing or transactional systems, as well as back-end analytics, which largely use historical data from the transactional systems combined with other internal and external data. The next frontier of analytics is in the predictive arena, not just mining data but applying statistical models to predict future behaviors or outcomes. It should also be noted that as analytics and predictive models are being embedded into operational processes for sales, underwriting, and other processes, the demand for real-time data access is increasing.

Figure 10-1 shows the most common business processes and related sub-processes in the Property and Casualty value chain. Each of these processes is further reviewed with a deeper description of these sub-processes in the sections that follow.

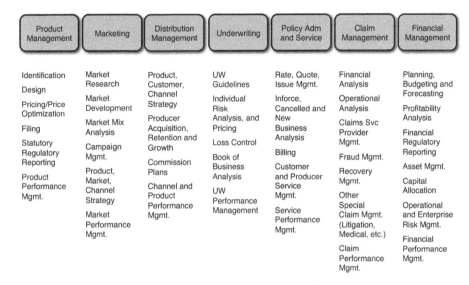

Product Management	Marketing	Distribution Management	Underwriting	Policy Adm and Service	Claim Management	Financial Management
Identification	Market Research	Product, Customer, Channel Strategy	UW Guidelines	Rate, Quote, Issue Mgmt.	Financial Analysis	Planning, Budgeting and Forecasting
Design	Market Development		Individual Risk Analysis, and Pricing	Inforce, Cancelled and New Business Analysis	Operational Analysis	Profitability Analysis
Pricing/Price Optimization	Market Mix Analysis	Producer Acquisition, Retention and Growth	Loss Control		Claims Svc Provider Mgmt.	Financial Regulatory Reporting
Filing	Campaign Mgmt.			Billing	Fraud Mgmt.	
Statutory Regulatory Reporting	Product, Market, Channel Strategy	Commission Plans	Book of Business Analysis	Customer and Producer Service Mgmt.	Recovery Mgmt.	Asset Mgmt.
Product Performance Mgmt.	Market Performance Mgmt.	Channel and Product Performance Mgmt.	UW Performance Management	Service Performance Mgmt.	Other Special Claim Mgmt. (Litigation, Medical, etc.)	Capital Allocation
					Claim Performance Mgmt.	Operational and Enterprise Risk Mgmt.
						Financial Performance Mgmt.

Figure 10-1 Insurance Industry Value Chain and Use Cases

Product Management

The Product management process includes target product identification, design, pricing, product filing, and product performance management including profitability. Pricing actuaries play a strong supporting role in the product management process especially in the pricing, product, and ongoing rate filings and state regulatory filing process. In some organizations, the product managers are not actuaries; in others they are. It has been said the actuarial area is the research and development function of an insurance company.

Price optimization is a key analytic used to help insurers attain the maximum volume at the highest price, or ideally, profitability. This function is often performed by pricing actuaries or by product managers or product analysts within the product area. Using statistical tools, a price optimization model uses pure premium, financial objectives, a rate model, anticipated cross-selling effects, and competitors rates as inputs and generates individual premiums optimized to meet an organization's policy or contract volume and profitability targets. These models can be used for new business as well as renewal. Some include *generalized linear modeling (GLM)*, an approach broadly used by actuaries. Most statistical tool vendors offer cross-industry price optimization models, which can be adapted for insurance based on a carrier's product mix and financial targets. Actuarial consulting firms also offer price optimization consulting.

Marketing

The *marketing management* process includes market research, market development, market mix optimization, campaign management, product market channel strategy, and overall marketing performance management. *Market mix optimization (MMO)* refers to marketing budget, spend and return across various channels, both traditional-print, email, TV, search and in-person events, as well as new digital, location-based, mobile, and social.

As part of the marketing function, companies define their overall markets (personal, commercial, specialty lines; group; and individual business), identify product categories, provide input on pricing strategies, define target customer markets and market segments (for example, preferred and standard), and align distribution channels and producers to sell their products with product managers.

Marketers measure and compare their overall marketing performance not only by market penetration but also by product and class of business profitability. They also review overall financial business performance internally and compare to their own historical performance as well as to the industry as a whole and to key competitors (peer performance).

An organization's marketing, underwriting, and distribution strategy should all be integrated and aligned. You don't want to market to customers that you would not ultimately underwrite. Doing so would be at the risk of mis-spending limited marketing dollars as well as alienating prospects and distribution partners.

Leading practices in marketing and market segmentation are all about data granularity and defining ever more detailed targets correlating to more rating and pricing cells for laser targeting. In the 90s, *Customer Relationship Management (CRM)* thought leaders Peppers and Rogers advocated one-to-one marketing. Although the insurance industry may not be at segments of one yet, it has certainly embraced more detailed segmentation enabled by the explosion of data that augments application data by more sophisticated use of analytics—especially statistical models—and by applying best practices from other industries such as banking and retail. Further they are incented to improve customer retention and cross-sell due to the front-loading of new business acquisition costs.

As part of marketing, insurers segment customers, define desired customer segments and characteristics, define products, and appoint agencies to sell to these customers. Insurers use external data to link customers in a "household" analysis to maximize wallet share not only for a single customer but also for all potential policyholders in a household. They also use statistical models to calculate potential customer *"life time value" (LTV)* and profitability; they use LTV concepts to define and present product offers at various key life stages or events, for example, birth, graduation from college, marriage, birth of a child, and divorce. They need to measure customer acquisition success, customer retention, customer growth, and customer profitability. Customer satisfaction is a key determinant of customer retention and growth.

Companies often conduct customer surveys to measure satisfaction and issues. Customer satisfaction is key to retention and even to new customer acquisition of third-party claimants who have had an exceptionally good claim experience.

Marketing is beginning to use social media and sentiment analysis. *Sentiment analysis* refers to positive and negative opinions detected through sentiment analytics (opinion mining) to identify negative and positive emotions.

Social media use has exploded, especially among the young. The top three web sites according to the eBizMBA Rank are Facebook with more than 900 million users, followed by Twitter with 290 million and LinkedIn with 250 million users. The top 10 insurers have taken notice and are looking to leverage social media for increased brand awareness as well as increased engagement with prospects, policyholders, and producers. But social media is a double-edged sword. Insurers are tuning into sentiment analysis tools to monitor sentiment in real time, leveraging particularly positive sentiment and "crises managing" extremely negative ones as soon as possible.

Customer Relationship Management

Customer Relationship Management (CRM) analytics are a class of marketing analytics unto themselves often delivered through a separate CRM analytics application, which includes customer profiling and segmentation as well as campaign management capabilities. CRM applications are not applied only to personal or individual lines marketing but can also be applied equally as well to small business or small group insurance. Individual customer characteristics such as age, income, occupation, and ethnicity (not race) can easily be translated to business characteristics of industry type, years in business, revenue, number of employees, and business type (such as female/women owned businesses). Health insurers have used a similar approach to CRM for Member Relationship Management (MRM) and *Provider Relationship Management (PRM)*.

Some organizations have outsourced their market analytics; however, this is such a critical analytic area that a wiser choice is to develop analytic capabilities in-house using consultants and services for knowledge transfer or to augment in-house capabilities.

The following case studies illustrate leadership in marketing.

CASE STUDY: PROGRESSIVE INSURANCE SETS THE STANDARD FOR P&C PERSONAL LINES SEGMENTATION

Progressive Insurance changed the game in personal auto in the 80s and 90s by using detailed data and statistics to define granular market segments and rating structures. Instead of the standard industry practice of using actuaries or rating bureaus to define its segments and pricing schema, it used statisticians. Using this statistical approach it found profitable opportunities within the substandard segments that previously most carriers avoided.

Leveraging statistical models even further, it integrated the models into its web-based quote tool and boldly displayed competitors rates even when Progressive's were not lower, driving business it did not want to its competitors and forcing competitors rates even lower. Using this approach Progressive reported results in one state that were 12 points better than its competitors.

CASE STUDY: PENN NATIONAL TAKES A PAGE FROM PROGRESSIVE

When Penn National was losing market share in New Jersey a few years ago due to a number of new competitors, including GEICO and Mercury, entering the personal auto market, it needed to make a quit or "invest to survive" decision. It opted to invest and undertook a major underwriting transformation that was analytics-driven, moving from class to risk underwriting and expanding from 3 rating tiers to 30.

The payoff was huge. It grew its personal lines business more than 100% and reduced underwriting expenses by $1 million in eliminating unnecessary motor vehicle reports (MVRs). It also increased its underwriting "straight through processing" rate on new business from 19% to more than 90% and significantly increased the efficiency of its underwriting renewal processing as well.

Market-basket analysis is an analytic technique commonly used in retail. The mythical "diapers and beer" was a result of market basket analysis. Convenience stores started stocking diapers next to the refrigerated cases with beer to up-sell young fathers who were making midnight diaper runs.

Zurich North American applied this technique to "force-rank" its U.S. small business book of business into high, medium, and low using two key dimensions: margin on premium and return on risk for capital allocation. Using this ranking approach it created 68 segments, which then enabled it to allocate its capital more effectively and execute appropriately on the small business segments that it wanted to grow, maintain, or shrink.

Sales and Distribution Management

The *distribution management* process includes an integrated product, customer, and channel strategy; producer acquisition, retention, and growth management; commission and incentive planning; and overall channel and product performance management. As stated earlier, an organization's marketing, underwriting, and distribution strategy should all be integrated and aligned.

As part of the marketing process, organizations align their customer segments and products to appropriate distribution channels, agencies/brokerage firms, and producers. They need to measure and compare channel performance both on a revenue and a profitability basis. Using analytics, they define territories, appoint agencies, adjust commission structures, and develop producer incentives. They continuously monitor and adjust these activities based on their goals and sales performance.

They closely watch to make sure their distribution force is "engaged," meaning actively bringing the volume and quality of business wanted by the insurer. As many producers look to carriers for leads, carriers are finding that they need to provide leads to keep them engaged.

CASE STUDY: CREATING A 360-DEGREE PRODUCER VIEW WITH EXTERNAL DATA

One carrier began augmenting its producer information with Dun & Bradstreet (D&B) data to measure and improve engagement. It compared revenue reported to D&B and pressed under-engaged producers on why they weren't getting sufficient revenue share.

D&B data also enabled the company to improve its producer "master data management" by linking subsidiaries and affiliates with a master producer code/name for a 360-degree producer view. Further, because most relationships and interactions are at the local office level, the organization filled gaps in contacts in its producer corporate headquarters contact names and ensured that its distribution partners' senior management were included for key field communications as well as the local or regional producers.

Similar to being used for CRM in marketing, insurers also use statistics and modeling to segment their agents, to attract, retain, and grow their business with them using techniques similar to those used in CRM applications. In fact, insurers have leveraged their CRM applications for *Distribution Relationship Management (DRM)*.

Incentive Compensation Management (ICM) is another analytics area that has evolved into a separate analytics application. ICM captures plan design; manages and administers compensation plans, quotas, crediting and adjustments; and supports commission statements and reports. Some insurers and vendors have modified this cross-industry sales analytics application for producer performance to calculate the effectiveness of commissions and incentives.

A large North American life and annuity insurer wanted to increase the productivity of its sales force. In phase one, it developed a set of dashboards for its internal sales management to review producer performance for business quoted, sold, and closed by region, office, and sales rep. Using this dashboard, it reviewed the business by time period and by product line, in-force versus new business, and so on. The insurer analyzed its producers by segments, for example, priority reps, large case reps, account managers, sales managers, and such.

It used this visibility into producer engagement and performance to improve coaching on executing and also developed enhancements to existing programs for wanted market penetration and growth. As a next phase of the project, the carrier developed tools for the producers to manage its own book of business including benchmarks on how it ranked versus it peers.

Underwriting

The *underwriting management* process includes defining underwriting guidelines for underwriters and producers; analyzing, classifying and pricing individual risks; developing and applying appropriate loss control/risk management programs; assessing its book of business/portfolio analysis; and reviewing overall underwriting performance. An organization's marketing, strategy, and distribution strategy should all be integrated and aligned.

Insurers define underwriting guidelines by product or product class and ultimately create strategic business units or profit centers by which they can measure their underwriting performance. Personal lines underwriting has become largely automated with manual underwriting conducted on an exception basis. Actuaries have become co-located within underwriting units in many P&C personal lines organizations, to be more agile in setting and modifying rates and pricing. In some commercial lines such as Workers Compensation, insurers have "scored" accounts for high, no, and low touch underwriting to improve underwriter ductivity, underwriting cycle/response time, and underwriting exper____.

The use of *credit scoring*, pioneered in banking for home loans, has been extensively applied in P&C personal lines insurance to augment or as a proxy for traditional underwriting criteria. Although behavioral, it has been effectively used to assess temperament and "morale" risk. It has also been used in life insurance, but not on as widespread a basis as in P&C. Credit scoring has been used in health insurance as well; however, under ObamaCare health insurers must take all applicants under guarantee issue and renewal rules, are subject to nondiscrimination rules, cannot apply pre-existing condition exclusions, and have rating restrictions or are using community instead of experience rating—all of which limit or repress traditional risk classification, evaluation, and pricing criteria.

Analytics are also used to streamline the underwriting process and reduce underwriting expenses, as the following examples illustrate.

CASE STUDY: UNDERWRITING EXPENSE REDUCTION

One P&C insurer found significant savings in property underwriting inspection expenses using analytics. Its long-standing underwriting procedure had been to conduct a property inspection on all new business. After analyzing its portfolio it realized the inspections had little impact on the quality of the risk for most of its business. It revised its guidelines to use inspections for certain high-value homes or risks with specific criteria, basically shifting to an 80/20 strategy; that is, ordering inspections on the 20% of policies where they matter. This underwriting process change resulted in a significant improvement in its underwriting profit due to these reduced underwriting expenses.

Life insurers are similarly beginning to analyze the impact of traditional tests ordered as part of the underwriting process for medical exams, lab tests, and so on. According to estimates in a study by the Society of Actuaries and Deloitte Consulting, the average cost of traditional underwriting expenses per applicant is $130, which can be reduced to $5 per applicant for certain segments. Based on 50,000 applications per year, potential savings are in the range of $2 million to $3 million—a compelling opportunity.

CASE STUDY: TELEMATICS AND USAGE-BASED INSURANCE

Insurers are leveraging telematics (telemetry + informatics) to more accurately evaluate, price, and manage risk based on actual insured behavior. In auto insurance, usage-based insurance (UBI) or pay as you drive (PAYD) insurance is based on driving behavior and other factors. Black boxes or on-board devices use vehicle data (from onboard computers), global system for mobile communication (GSM) data, and global positioning systems (GPS) data with predictive models as elements of usage derived risk pricing. "Pure play" UBI insurers are emerging; these carriers' business models are based on a UBI rating and underwriting approach.

In the United States, Progressive Insurance has again taken a lead in UBI for personal auto, but other carriers including Allstate, State Farm, and USAA have followed form rapidly. UBI is becoming broadly used in Europe, especially in Italy, which was one of the first adopters. Commercial lines carriers are also applying telematics; Allianz and Zurich are using telematics globally for Commercial Auto Fleet insurance and risk management, driver safety training, and loss prevention. Telematics are also emerging for use in home insurance using "smart home" technologies, as well as in other property lines. Inland and Ocean Marine insurers are tracking cargo inside truck and ships using radio frequency identification devices (RFID) tags. They are also used in claims management for stolen vehicle recovery.

In health insurance, telematics have been applied accessing data from medical devices such as glucose monitors and fitness monitors for use in increasingly mobile health and wellness programs and applications. With the increasing automation of administrative, financial, and clinical systems such as computerized patient order entry (CPOE), electronic medical records (EMR), and other applications in healthcare, integration of data from these transactional systems combined with pharmacy data and other data sources will lead to more sophisticated and more proactive health and wellness programs—especially in view of the recent accountable care organization healthcare delivery model trend. Potential applications abound for both insurance and risk management, across sectors.

Policy/Contract Administration and Service

The *policy/contract administration and service management* process involves managing application processing/enrollment; rating and producing quotes and issuing policy/contact if accepted along with appropriate identity cards; billing and premium collection for the policy/contract; processing policy renewals, nonrenewals or cancellations; providing administrative support to customers and/or producers through the policy/contract life cycle; and reviewing overall service performance management.

These services are largely provided through a call center; although, increasingly they are delivered by multiple channels including in-person (by agent or field service offices), web, and mobile.

Service management analytics, sometimes referred to as *call center* or *customer interaction center analytics,* are used to ensure that customer and producer requests are fulfilled in a timely manner and to ensure that enough service center resources are available to meet demand. They measure call wait times, length of call, number of transfers, and so on. Insurers are using this data not only to evaluate the performance of its service center reps, but also to improve overall service capabilities, which leads to increased customer, member and producer satisfaction, and ultimately retention.

Insurers also conduct customer and producer satisfaction surveys, review complaints, and use analysis to modify their administrative and service management strategies as well as products. Increasingly insurers are using social media and *Sentiment Analysis* applications, which measure attitudes and behaviors, to measure customer and producer satisfaction.

CASE STUDY: LEVERAGING CUSTOMER SERVICE TO INCREASE CUSTOMER RETENTION AND WALLET SHARE

In the late 1990s, most property and casualty insurance companies left the majority of customer service interactions to their agents. However, as Internet and call center technologies improved, insurers began taking service back in-house, initially driven by reducing sales commissions for service.

One large national P&C organization based in the Northeast found through using analytics that not only could it deliver customer service more cost-effectively and efficiently, leading to increased customer satisfaction and retention, but it improved its producers' ability to up-sell and cross-sell existing customers as well as focus on new business. Another benefit this company realized was the capability to collect customer feedback directly, which led to improved and new product development.

Producers are increasingly looking to insurers to leverage their massive data sets and analytics capabilities to provide leads; providing analysis (lead lists and best practices) and analytical applications (dashboards, scorecards, and such) to producers is affecting carriers mind share with producers.

Claims

The *claims management* process includes first notice of loss, intake, or claim filing; claims registry and reserving; claim review, investigation/assessment and payout/settlement or defense; claim payment recovery; specialty claim handling such as litigation management, medical management, and so on; and overall Claims Performance Management.

First and foremost the primary goal of every insurer is prompt, fair settlement of covered claims. Claims are often described as the ultimate "moment of truth" for a policyholder. Beyond the initial policy issuance, the only direct customer touch point for most insureds is through a claim interaction, so the perceived quality of claim service is critical to retention. New business has even been driven through outstanding claims service to a third-party claimant. Quality claim service is not just a good business practice; carriers are subject to Fair Claims Practices laws. In some states, fines and penalties may incur for a late claim payment, especially in health insurance.

Insurers develop claim administration guidelines to ensure customers receive prompt and fair claim services. They may need to re-allocate staff or as in P&C hire independent adjusters during a catastrophic event like a hurricane. They measure their claim performance both for effectiveness and efficiency. Claims operational efficiency measures include the number of open claims, claim cycle time, customer claim satisfaction, staff turnover, and so on. Claims financial effectiveness measures include incurred, reserves, paid amounts, cost to adjust, legal fees, and such.

Losses (indemnity payments) in property and casualty as well as health insurance on average represent 75% of the premium dollar; they are essentially to insurance what Cost of Goods Sold is to other industries.

Loss reserving analytics in the form of loss trending (loss development triangles or "loss ladders") is a key analysis usually performed by actuaries. It is used to review so called "long tail" loss development over the course of 10+ years. This applies to Property and Casualty Liability or Workers Compensation lines of business and is used for pricing and loss reserving.

Loss exposure analysis is conducted on a more immediate basis by claims analysts, underwriters, and loss control specialists looking for potential emerging loss exposures and accident or injury patterns. Loss control specialists look for common injuries or causes of loss and work with underwriters to improve loss prevention or mitigation strategies.

Underwriters especially closely watch claims on new products. Because these are often new exposures and are not captured in a coded cause of loss field or are captured in an "all other" category, using text analysis on description of loss fields is valuable. Even on mature products new exposures can develop, such as toxic mold. Some carriers noted the toxic mold exposure by mining the text data in the loss descriptions and increased deductibles and limited damages from mold earlier than their peers.

Claims fraud analysis is a key analytic used across all three segments. Fraud is involved in 10% of all claims, which translates to $80 billion; hence insurers aggressively address claim fraud. They have dedicated Special Investigation Units (SIUs), which investigate potential fraudulent claims referred by claims adjusters or through automated business rules as part of initial loss processing before they even pay a claim. Some insurers have leveraged their fraud models even further by embedding rules into their underwriting systems to detect potential first-party fraud before a policy is even written. Insurers are also starting to take advantage of social media to contest claimants disability claims, for example, a claimant who cannot perform his daily work but is seen putting a new roof on his house.

CASE STUDY: FRAUDSTERS BEWARE— BIG BROTHER IS WATCHING

An insurer was suspicious about an automobile claim involving a high value luxury vehicle that was driven into a lake, allegedly due to a large bird flying into the driver's path. An intrepid fraud examiner successfully declined the claim after finding a serendipitous YouTube video showing the vehicle driven into the lake, clearly showing the absence of any such flying bird.

Some workers compensation and disability carriers are similarly using social media that contradicts and shows claimants performing activities beyond their alleged disabilities, for example, painting their house, bowling, or skiing.

Claims recoveries is another area that uses analytics. Claims recovery analysts seek to maximize claims payment recoveries from salvage, subrogation, reinsurance, Workers Compensation Second Injury Funds, and other sources. Additional third-party sources include manufacturers' warranties. The following example shows how claims analysts identified potential recoveries.

CASE STUDY: SUV ROLLOVERS AND FAULTY TIRES

When sports utility vehicles (SUVs) first appeared in the U.S. market, insurers noted a high incidence of roll-over accidents. Adjusters, underwriters, and loss control reps struggled to understand the cause of loss. Was it the vehicle? Was it driver behavior? Digging through their claims data, they began to find patterns. One pattern that emerged was vehicle models with specific tire manufacturers. Insurers pursued claims recoveries against these manufacturers. They searched their databases for prior paid claims using the year and vehicles' IDs to find potential recoveries.

Similar recoveries have been pursued against kitchen appliance manufacturers for fire losses that originated in stoves and dishwashers; recall data and warranty data were used to find these opportunities.

Finance

The *financial management* process includes budgeting, planning, and forecasting; profitability analysis; financial and statutory regulatory reporting; management reporting; asset management; capital analysis and allocation; operational and enterprise risk management including reinsurance management; and overall finance risk management.

Insurers measure overall *Enterprise Performance Management (EPM),* also called *corporate performance management (CPM)* for growth and profitability. They analyze premiums, losses, expenses, and profitability on an enterprise, line of business, product, and regional basis. Some of this analysis is done daily (premiums); other analytics are conducted weekly, monthly, quarterly, or annually.

Planning and budgeting (and forecasting) has become an analytic application that measures actual versus targeted (budgeted) metrics. Leading practices include using rolling 18-month forecasts versus static 12-month ones and employ *driver-based planning* approaches. For example, key drivers for auto premiums could include the number of new cars sold, auto parts prices, and so on. Planning and budgeting also produces a number of standard performance management reports such as income statements, balance sheets, and profit and loss reports. Increasingly they are including daily management scorecards with drill down into detail data to provide timely insight into performance and enable the opportunity to change tactics to ensure meeting targets.

Activity-Based Costing (ABC), or *Cost Accounting,* is also an analytic application that is sometimes integrated within an overall EPM Suite along with the planning and budgeting application. ABC measures the effect of cost drivers and is often a key component of a profitability analysis application. Insurers have used ABC to analyze process cost drivers to reduce expenses. *Sensitivity analysis*, or what-if analysis, is often included as part of ABC applications to evaluate the impact of adjusting cost drivers.

External and Internal Reporting

From an external reporting perspective, insurers prepare regulatory, statutory, and stakeholder reporting.

- All insurers need to comply with quarterly and annual state regulatory (statutory) reporting requirements as well as ad hoc state and other regulatory reporting requests. These requirements and requests are usually fulfilled in the actuarial area.

- Public companies need to comply with the appropriate regulatory agency (for example, United States SEC) requirements also typically on a quarterly and annual basis. These requirements are usually fulfilled in the finance area.

- Investor relations fulfills and coordinates annual reports, presentations, and other content for investors, stock analysts, and other stakeholders.

- Nonpublic companies usually also need to create reports to members or other nonshareholder stakeholders. These reports are also usually fulfilled in finance.

Internal (management) reports are also prepared for monthly, quarterly, and annual profit and loss reports and other corporate performance management, as well as board packages (key summarized executive reports).

XBRL (extended business reporting language), which is XML for reporting, can simplify financial report production using standard taxonomies. XBRL is used globally across a wide range of sectors, including securities regulation, banking, insurance, data aggregators, and taxation, as well as for nonfinancial reporting such as carbon disclosure, sustainability efforts, and risk reporting.

XBRL has already been adopted for International Financial Reporting Standards (IFRS), US GAAP, and European Solvency II, and is considered for other reporting purposes. XBRL provides benefits at all stages of business reporting and analysis, in automation; cost-saving; faster, more reliable, and more accurate handling of data; improved analysis; and in better quality of information and decision-making. More information and a complete list of approved and pending taxonomies can be found at www.xbrl.org.

CASE STUDY: C N A FINANCIAL DATA WAREHOUSE

In the 2000s, C N A Insurance underwent a significant business transformation driven by a new senior management team. Previously, it had been a multiline carrier writing both property-casualty and life-health insurance business. C N A exited the life business and also sold off its property-casualty personal lines book of business to focus on commercial and specialty lines.

To support this transformation and ensure meeting its profitability targets, C N A developed a Finance Data Warehouse that initially included summary Key Performance Indicators (KPIs). Over time, the Finance Data Warehouse expanded to include detail data and has grown into an Enterprise Data Warehouse supported by Strategic Governance leadership and processes supporting finance, actuarial, claims, risk control, and other operational areas. Business ownership for the data warehouse and the BI strategy falls under a Shared Services Information group in finance that works closely with C N A's IT leadership. This Shared Service Information management area includes a strong data governance focus to ensure data quality, data confidence, and data usability.

C N A derived a number of benefits including reduced expense associated with compiling information and scrubbing data. Full integration of planning and budgeting and actuals allowed C N A to focus on areas that required attention resulting in lower expenses, improved loss ratios, and growth. Strategies supporting loss reduction and growth were accelerated through better information.

Enterprise Risk Management (ERM)

Enterprise risk management (ERM) is the process of planning, organizing, leading, and controlling the activities of an organization to minimize the effects of risk on an organization's capital and earnings. It includes all risks—hazard (underwriting), financial, strategic, and operational risk. This function is headed by a chief risk officer (CRO), often an actuary, who works with the CFO, CEO, and board to define, manage, and monitor an insurer's ERM strategy. Actuarial professional associations including the Casualty Actuarial Society (CAS) and Society of Actuaries (SOA) have provided ERM forums for thought leadership in this critical function.

ERM applications support this strategy. The ability to aggregate and normalize data from multiple data sources including operational and financial systems is a critical component. This integration of risk and finance data supports understanding risks relative to business objectives and overall business performance. ERM applications also help insurers improve and address compliance with ever-increasing regulatory risk reporting and also improve senior management and the board's role in oversight.

ERM applications include the ability to extract data in an automated, controlled way from multiple source systems into an integrated risk register. Scenario analysis is used to predict losses using internal and external data. Risk analytics, reports, and alerts to support decision making are also included as well as compliance-related functions, such as audit trails, regulatory reporting, or control policy. ERM applications are increasingly part of *governance, risk (management)*, and *compliance (GRC)* suites.

Reinsurance analysis is part of an overall ERM program and involves reviewing overall corporate exposures, done both at the individual risk level and the aggregate level. Individual risk reinsurance is part of the underwriting process and handled with facultative reinsurance. Aggregate reinsurance exposures are predicted and addressed via corporate reinsurance programs.

Catastrophe exposure analysis is also part of ERM analysis; it involves the use of catastrophe risk models to estimate the losses from a catastrophic event such as a hurricane or earthquake. In P&C, catastrophe modeling involves a confluence of actuarial science, engineering, and meteorology. In health insurance, similar models are used to predict pandemics and other significant mortality events or losses. Carriers are using ever more sophisticated risk models to predict future catastrophic losses and then determine how they will allocate capital as part of their overall market strategy as well as financial risk management of actual losses. Reinsurance is one alternative to address these exposures; others include retention or alternative risk shifting to a mechanism such as catastrophe bonds.

Insurers typically have an ERM department with actuarial and financial analysts who produce these analytics. Some insurers use actuarial or ERM consulting firms in lieu of their own analysts or to augment them.

Health Insurance Analytics

The value chain or business processes for health insurance includes all the same functions as property and casualty insurance, plus two more key areas unique to clinical analytics: *disease and wellness management* and *provider management.* Many of these clinical analytics are performed by medical affairs analysts, healthcare informatics analysts, and biostatisticians. It should also be noted that many similar processes are applied in P&C insurance in medical management in workers compensation and in catastrophic medical claims incurred, which are covered by auto, general liability, or other insurance.

The U.S. Patient Protection and Affordable Care Act (PPACA) is just being rolled out; the ramifications are yet to be known, but it is expected to have a profound impact on health insurance. The act requires health plans to accept all applicants and confines rating approach alternatives, leaving insurers with limited tools such as deductibles, co-payments to apply in risk assessment, pricing, and underwriting. Insurers are expected to leverage disease and wellness management to incent members to maintain their health and network provider management to insure cost-conscious and cost-effective providers. Fraud management programs used to detect fraud or billing abuses (unbundling medical procedure billings) are also expected to increase use of more sophisticated analysis, technologies, and more data sources in overall efforts to sustain profitability.

Disease and Wellness Management

Disease and wellness management, also called *population health management,* addresses wellness at different phases of the healthcare continuum. Proactive wellness and health management focus on disease prevention and keeping members healthy. Disease and case management focus on managing a member's existing health condition, especially those suffering from chronic conditions. According to the Centers for Disease Control and Prevention (CDC), chronic diseases account for about 75% of the U.S. aggregate healthcare spending. The top five diseases are heart disease, cancer, stroke, chronic pulmonary disorder, and diabetes. The key objectives of disease management programs are education, awareness, and improved behavior modification such as prescription adherence. The programs use incentives and tools to achieve these goals.

Analytics are a key component used to design and measure the efficacy of health and wellness management programs. Many of the same segmentation techniques used in marketing are also used to segment members for program participation. Behavioral analysis is used to determine which members are most likely to not adhere to taking their medications or follow protocols and to allocate limited "wellness" coach resources. Health insurers use internal claim information as well as external clinical data to define, administer, and manage effective health and wellness programs.

Utilization management (UM) is a subset of disease and wellness management; it analyzes procedures/services used by health population segments, which services used were in or out of network, average, total costs, and so on. These analyses are used both internally for effectiveness and efficiency review as part of population health management and provider management and externally by plan sponsors (employers) to review their overall plan design and cost management.

Provider and Network Management

Health insurers use claims data and member data to manage their provider networks including setting reimbursement rates for procedures and to ensure that they have the right mix of providers and specialists in their healthcare delivery networks to meet member needs. They also conduct benchmarking on costs and outcomes as part of Pay for Performance (P4P) programs to incent and reward providers. Some insurers are part of an integrated delivery network (IDN), meaning that they are both a payer and a provider, such as Kaiser Permanente. In addition, many organizations are looking at adopting the accountable health organization (ACO) business model to control their medical costs.

Many analytic approaches used for CRM and distribution relationship management, for example, segmentation, acquisition, engagement, retention, and growth, are also used in *provider relationship management (PRM)*.

CASE STUDY: UNITEDHEALTH GROUP'S NETWORK MANAGEMENT

The health insurance business is rapidly changing under the U.S. Patient Protection and Affordable Care Act (PPACA), more commonly referred to as the Affordable Care Act (ACA) or ObamaCare. Health Plans are reviewing and realigning their networks to meet requirements of the new plans. The law requires insurers to cover all applicants with new minimum plan standards and to offer the same premium rate regardless of pre-existing condition, sex, or other characteristics—using community versus experience rating.

UnitedHealth Group (UHG), one of the largest Medicare Advantage insurers in the United States, started changing its provider network in a number of states. UHG issued notices to members advising that it was dropping some doctors from its network and issued contract cancellations to those providers. In Connecticut, where reportedly 810 primary care and more than 1,400 specialists were affected, these actions created a backlash from both providers and members and complaints to state insurance departments and Medicare.

In response, Medicare issued a statement advising that it is giving scrutiny to UHG's as well as other health plans' provider networks and will be monitoring areas that have experienced "disruption" to ensure that members and beneficiaries have "full, transparent, and timely information and access to care." Clearly analytics will play a key ongoing role as these new plans roll out in 2014 and beyond.

Life Insurance Analytics

The life and annuity business is driven by two key levers, sales and investments. This industry segment has all the same basic business processes as the P&C segment, with less focus on claims operational efficiency because claims volume is generally much lower.

Unlike most property and casualty personal lines products, life, annuity, long-term health, and supplementary disability are not mandated by state law (auto insurance) or lenders (homeowners insurance). It has been said that "insurance is sold, not bought;" this is certainly true for these lines of business. Further, the recent economic market has had a significant negative impact on profit margins, lapse and surrender rates, and producer/advisor retention.

Analytics have been applied to address expense reduction, portfolio performance, profitability, and customer retention using both internal data, such as policyholder application data, and medical history. External data sources are also used in the form of psychographic/lifestyle, household, and even social media to augment internal data. Predictive models using behavioral analysis are used for lapse analysis to determine not only who will lapse, but also what key events are likely to trigger a lapse and to proactively avert them. Models are also used in surrender analysis to detect and prevent surrender using policy loans or to offer product alternatives instead of surrender.

The use of credit scores commonly used in P&C is still emerging in life insurance. Opportunities for more granular risk segmentation using external data and credit scores offer opportunity in life, annuity, long-term care, and disability insurance marketing, underwriting, and pricing. Similarly claims data is not leveraged as extensively for pricing analysis as the volume of life insurance claims is much less than in P&C.

Insurance company investments for all sectors are managed by the chief investment officer in the finance area. Premium and loss reserve investment options are restricted by state insurance law. For all insurers; policyholder surplus reserves have flexibility. CIOs often work with insurance industry-specific asset, risk, and capital management advisors or consulting firms to manage and optimize return on their overall investment and asset portfolio. In addition, life and annuity insurers are subject to "separate account" regulations, which require a fund maintained separately from an insurer's general assets; this requirement originated in response to federal securities laws for investment-linked variable annuities.

Summary

Learning Objectives

Test your basic knowledge of the main points in this chapter by answering the following questions:

- Understand the key business processes in P&C, life, and health insurance and key analytics by process.

- Review how analytics improve business processes and business performance,

Discussion Questions

Further check your application of key concepts by reviewing the following discussion questions:

- Name four key analytic categories used across all insurance industry segments.

- Identify two key examples of clinical analytics used in health insurance.

- Compare differences in use of analytics in underwriting (credit scoring) and claims management (volume of claims data) for P&C personal lines versus individual life insurance.

Key Terms

Customer Relationship Management (CRM) is the combination of processes and technologies that an organization uses to manage its customer relationships.

Distribution Relationship Management (DRM) is the combination of processes and technologies that an organization uses to manage its distribution partner relationships and channels.

Enterprise Performance Management (EPM), also sometimes called corporate performance management, refers to the combination of processes and technologies that an organization sues to manage its overall financial performance including planning and budgeting, and profitability analysis, financial consolidation, and strategic planning.

Enterprise Risk Management (EPM) is the combination of processes and technologies that an organization uses to manage and control its risks across the organization including strategic, operational, financial, and hazard (that is, underwriting) risks.

Healthcare informatics refers to the uses of biomedical data, information, and knowledge for scientific inquiry, problem solving, and decision making used to improve human health. It is sometimes referred to as *biomedical informatics* as the broad baseline discipline, *health informatics* when used to capture applied research and practice in clinical and public health informatics, and *medical informatics* when used in disease and wellness management.

Life Time Value (LTV) is a key analytic used in marketing to predict the net profit of a customer over the end-to-end course of a relationship. It calculates the present value of projected cash flows during the overall relationship life span.

Market Basket Analysis, also known as *affinity analysis*, is a data mining application that explores the likelihood of activities performed concurrently, for example, purchases. Largely used in retail to examine potential customer purchase behavior for cross-sell and up-sell, sales promotions, product placement, loyalty programs, and discount plans.

Marketing Mix Optimization uses statistical analysis against sales and marketing data to predict the impact of a current marketing mix of tactics for sales and also forecasts the impact of future sets of tactics. It is used to optimize advertising spend mix and promotional tactics for sales and profitability.

Population Health Management (Health and Wellness Management) is the combination of processes and technologies that an organization uses to manage its member health. It includes both preventative (wellness) and disease management.

Price optimization uses statistical models to calculate how demand varies at different price levels and combines those outcomes with information on costs and supply to recommend prices that will improve profits. It is used to define pricing for customer segments simulating how targeted customers will respond to price changes based on various data-driven scenarios. They help forecast demand, develop pricing and promotion strategies, control inventory levels, and improve customer satisfaction.

Psychographic data refers to data about personality, values, attitudes, interests, and lifestyles. It is often combined with demographic data and used for marketing analysis for buying behavior analysis.

Sentiment analysis, also known as opinion mining, is a data mining technique using a natural language process (NLP), text analysis, and computational linguistics to identify negative and positive emotions.

Text analytics uses text mining to derive meaning from unstructured data contained in natural language text in word documents, email, social media postings, and so on. It uses natural language processing (NLP), statistical modeling, and machine learning techniques.

Additional Resources/Reading

eBizMBA Rank Link www.ebizmba.com includes a ranking of top 10 social media sites.

"Predictive Modeling for Life Insurance," Society of Actuaries & Deloitte Consulting. April 2010. (A white paper).

"Predictive Modeling for Life Insurance: Ways Life Insurers Can Participate in the Business Analytics Revolution." Society of Actuaries. May 2012. (A presentation).

Professional Associations

AHIP (America's Insurance Health Plans) www.ahip.org.

AHIMA (American Health Information Management Association) www.ahima.org.

CAS (Casualty Actuarial Society) www.casact.org.

HIMSS (Health Information Management & Systems Society) www.himss.org.

IASA (Insurance Accounting and Statistical Assn.) www.iasa.org.

IMCA (Insurance Marketing Communication Association) www.imca.org.

SOA (Society of Actuaries) www.soa.org.

SIR (Society of Insurance Research) www.sirnet.org.

11

Future of Insurance Analytics

The insurance industry has long used analytics in many areas. However, there has not been an integrated, strategic approach to its use. Insurance has often been called a laggard in its use of technology overall and somewhat justifiably so; however, when proven many companies become fast adopters. The problem is that the last companies to adopt innovations, be they in technologies or analytic applications, do so at the peril of being marginalized and acquired by another company.

This chapter advocates some actions to advance your analytic maturity including analytic innovation tactics, conducting an analytic audit, and undertaking business discovery. A combination of these can help you retake a proactive approach to analytics so that you do not become marginalized.

Analytic Innovation Tactics

Following are some tactics that insurers can take to ensure they are not at peril.

- **Innovate with analytics: Think outside the box**

  Look for opportunities to innovate with analytics. Review new product development and market opportunities with an eye to apply analytics for innovation. Make analytics a part of new business plans development; identify areas in which analytics help identify, target, and realize new opportunities and value.

Many organizations use design thinking approaches for business plan development. This approach uses design principles combined with system thinking in an empathic approach to new processes, new applications, and new customer perspectives.

- **Think differently: Look outside the insurance industry**.

Some of the most promising applications in insurance come from other industries; telematics from automotive industry is now applied to usage-based insurance.

- **Strategic alignment: Align analytics with strategic planning and key initiatives.** As you conduct annual strategic planning and define initiatives, make sure that analytics are part of your plans. Think about how analytics can support your key objectives and what KPIs you need to measure your progress, and what data is needed for targeting and measuring your progress.

- **Put your analytics to work: Embed analytics into business processes**.

Put your analytics to work; apply them within your business processes. Analytics should make your operational systems smarter.

- **(Continue to) invest in analytics**

All too often insurers stop analytics initiatives or choose not to start them in deference to investing in upgrading or replacing transactional systems. Analytics are not an either/or strategy. You need BOTH transactional and analytic investments. Often you collect new data as part of a functional transformation project; you want to leverage that new data and gain insights from it.

- **Foster an analytics culture**

Not everyone has to be a data scientist, but every employee should have analytic curiosity. Encourage and support employees' personal development via training, projects, and external professional organizations.

Most professional associations have added analytics in some form to their professional designation curricula or educational programs including the Casualty Actuarial Society, Society of Actuaries, and Society of Chartered Property Casualty Underwriters.

The Society of Insurance Research has included analytics as a part of its annual conferences, regional workshops, and webinars for insurance professionals in marketing, market research, and product development. Many other professional organizations have done similarly.

- **Embrace new technologies**

  Start small; embrace proof of concepts and prototypes. Use cloud-hosted environments to avoid disruption of your existing in-house platforms. Use analytic "side-car" data store to serve up real-time data from your main data warehouse instead of impacting the performance and cost of your existing analytic environment. (They are called side-cars because they sit alongside your main data warehouse/data store.)

  Outsource emerging analytic applications to consultants; include knowledge transfer as part of your project plan and then bring your apps back in-house.

- **Embrace your Data—big and small**

  Build Big Data pilots to leverage new data like social media. Big Data is a valuable concept, and insurers should start using analytics sand boxes (labs) to experiment with new data types on "skunk works" projects as proof of concepts.

  But also use the traditional data that you already have. Invest in data governance and data quality initiatives to ensure you get the value from your existing data and develop good data hygiene and habits.

  If you do not have a formal data governance program, push to develop one. Your analytics are only as good as the quality of your data.

Analytics Audit

Many insurers use analytics, but they approach them tactically. Make sure that you have a 2 to 3 years Strategic Analytics Roadmap and that your analytics mission and roadmap are transparent. This can help drive your analytic culture and get people on-board using analytics and committing their time to projects that leverage them. Do a self-audit by asking yourself the following questions to validate whether you truly have an analytic strategy:

- **Business Analytics or BI Competency Center (BACC/BICC) or Center of Excellence (CoE):** Do you have a BI Center of Excellence/BI Competency Center?

  A formalized governance program for your BI/Analytics program.

- **Analytics executive sponsor or champion:** Do you have a chief analytics officer/chief data officer?

  If not in title, then in principle. Could be the SVP, Strategy. This is a senior business leader who is the sponsor or champion for analytics.

- **Complete BI strategy:** Do you have a BI strategy that goes beyond an architecture diagram and technology?

  Your architecture chart is only one element of your strategy. You need a requirements process, business value process, and overarching governance process as well as an information and technology infrastructure.

- **Self-service BI/analytics:** Do you have self-service BI/analytics capabilities?

  Are you getting the analytics you need—on a timely basis so that they can help you make decisions? Can you explore data without IT intervention? IT cannot possibly meet all the current needs and growing needs for analytics.

  You need to have a self-service analytics strategy and governance. This is not just about the tools; it's about user skills, data access, and more.

- **Mobile strategy:** Do you have a mobile BI strategy?

  Can you access BI reports and dashboards from mobile devices? Have you defined who needs access to mobile BI: employees, partners, customers, and the applications that they need? Have you looked at mobile device standards and data security?

- **External use of analytics:** Does your BI strategy extend beyond the enterprise to your producers, policyholders, and providers/business partners?

  What BI capabilities/apps/data do you want to make accessible to policyholders, producers, and partners? (Not limited to mobile).

- **Analytic maturity:** Do you have analytics beyond just reporting or dashboards?

  Are your analytics accessible by employees other than statisticians or actuaries? What is the state of your analytic maturity? What are your goals to evolve? What challenges are keeping you from evolving? What's your plan to overcome them?

- **Social media/sentiment analysis:** Do you use social media and sentiment analysis?

  Are you starting to leverage social media? How are you going to integrate the data? Are you doing text mining? Do you have the right tools? Do you need training?

- **External data:** Are you leveraging external data as well as internal data?

  How can you integrate internal and external data? How are you managing third-party data subscriptions?

- **Metrics and KPIs:** Do you have a metrics framework?

  Do you know the top 20 metrics that measure your organization's success? And not just regulatory reporting metrics. By functional area. How do they roll up to summary metrics? Have you identified the leading indicators for these KPIs?

- **Real-Time analytics:** Do you have real-time analytics where you need them?

   Not all analytics needs to be real time, but some do. Have you identified where they are needed? For example, next best sales offers, fraud, and so on.

BI Strategy Alignment and Feasibility

Understanding business needs, prioritizing them in terms of business value and evaluating their feasibility are three keys to your analytic success. A business discovery is the most common approach used to validate your analytic needs, value, and feasibility.

Conduct a Business Discovery

To ensure that your BI strategy is business-aligned, conduct a business discovery. This approach analyzes and compares future and current business needs and capabilities and identifies gaps; it also measures value to business to prioritize addressing gaps and future needs. Lastly, it examines feasibility. The process engages and aligns business and IT. The following are questions that can be posed to define both current and future needs, and current capability gaps.

Current/Future Needs
- What are the top two to three business initiatives for your area? (By functional area)
- For each initiative what analytics will be critical to help deliver and measure the success of these initiatives?
- What are your current BI challenges (access to data, data quality, data completeness, delay in delivery of requested analytics, and so on)?

Business Value
- What would you do differently if you had these analytics or insight?
- How would you apply them to your business processes?

- How would they improve your business performance—increased revenue, reduced expenses, and lower risk? How would you measure this improvement?

- What KPIs would you use to measure this progress?

- What is the relative value—high, medium or low, relative to other analytics initiatives?

Feasibility

- Do you have the data you need for these analytics? If not, what is missing? Can you get it elsewhere?

- Do you have reports or tools to expose these analytics? Do you have the skills to generate them?

- What other hurdles are you facing? (Data quality, data access, data currentness, skills, authority to act on the data, and so on)

It is an ever-changing world in which more people, things, and activities are interconnected and empowered by analytics. Organizations that practice continuous awareness, education, and improvement in the application of analytics within their organizations can enable them to deliver true value by helping members and policyholders to live healthier, wealthier, and safer lives.

Recommended Reading/Additional Resources

"Advances that will transform life, business, and the global economy." White Paper. McKinsey & Co. May 2013.

Mayer-Schönberger, Viktor and Kenneth Cukier. *Big Data: A Revolution That Will Transform How We Live, Work, and Think.* Houghton Mifflin Harcourt, 2013.

Davenport, Tom. *Big Data@Work. Dispelling the Myths, Uncovering the Opportunities.* Harvard Business School Publishing, 2014.

"The Global Innovation 1000. Navigating the Digital Future." Study. Booz & Co. 2013. *Strategy+Business.* www.strategy-buisness.com.

"Insurance Tech Trends 2013. Elements of postdigital." White Paper. Deloitte Development LLC. 2013.

Gurin, Joel. *Open Data Now: The Secret to Hot Startups, Smart Investing, Savvy Marketing, and Fast Innovation.* McGraw-Hill, 2014.

Gunther, Rita. *The End of Competitive Advantage: How to Keep Your Strategy Moving as Fast as Your Business.* Harvard Business Publishing. 2013.

Harvard Business Review. www.harvardbusinessreview.com. Harvard Business Publishing.

McKinsey Quarterly. www.mckinsey.com. McKinsey & Co.

Strategy + Business magazine. www.strategy-business.com. Booz & Co.

Events/Forums

ACORD-IDMA. Insurance Data & Analytics Summit. www.acord.org.

ACORD-LOMA Annual Conference. www.acord.org.

Casualty Actuarial Society. Ratemaking (Predictive Modeling) & Product Management Forum. www.casact.org.

Enterprise Risk Management Symposium. www.ermsymposium.org.

HIMSS Annual Conference. www.himss.org.

Insurance & Data Management Association Annual Conference. www.idma.org.

International Institute for Analytics Chief Annual Analytic Officer Summit. www.iianalytics.com.

Society of Actuaries. Advanced Business Analytics. www.soa.org.

Society of Insurance Research. Annual Conference. www.sirnet.org.

A

Analytics Evolution Models

You can use the following models in Figures A–1 and A–2 to help evaluate and compare your company's analytics maturity relative to the industry as a whole. The dots indicate the industry maturity.

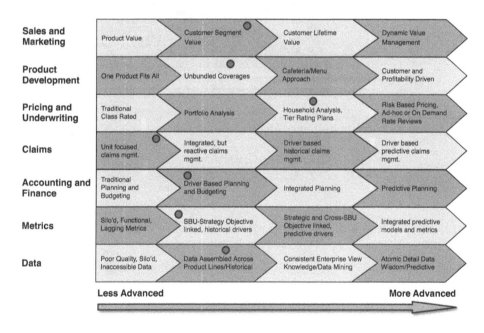

Figure A–1 Property and Casualty/Life Insurance Analytics Evolution

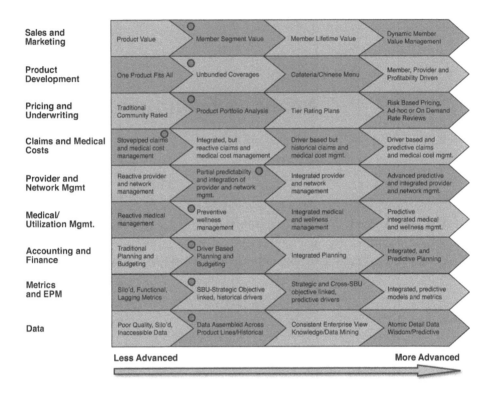

Figure A-2 Health Insurance Analytics Evolution

B

Actionability and Metrics Frameworks

The following frameworks in Figures B-1 through B-10 have been included to help you define and validate analytic actionability and to define key metrics and dimensions.

Objective	Business Questions/Analysis	Actions	Measureable Results and KPIs
Increase Profitable Growth (Market Share and Profitability)	■ How can we align agents and customers for profitability? Which are our most profitable channels, agencies and producers? What are our sales costs by Channel? Touch point? Activity? ■ What impact does commissions, other incentives have on sales performance? ■ How can we optimize our most effective agents' productivity? How can we reduce our selling costs? Which administrative tasks can we move from agents to our call centers? ■ What is the quality (profitability) of the business we are receiving from our distribution? What desirable business are we not receiving? Why?	■ Plan strategies to optimize channel and agency alignment ■ Optimize channel and agent productivity ■ Shift activities to lower cost channels ■ Review and update channel, agency incentives	■ Meet channel, agency and producer volume and revenue goals (policies per customer/ household, written premiums, etc.) ■ Increased market share in target segments ■ Reduced sales costs ■ Improved profitability
Agent and Customer Satisfaction and Retention	■ What are our new business trends? (new applications/submissions, quotes, policies issued) ■ What are our renewals trends? (renewals, cancellations, non-renewals), ■ What is our customer and agent satisfaction with our products, pricing and service? What are their retention rates?	■ ID and analyze negative new business trends and take action ■ ID and analyze negative renewal trends and take action ■ ID and analyze negative satisfaction trends and take action	■ Meeting new business and renewal goals ■ Improved customer and agent satisfaction ■ Improved customer and agent retention
Associate Retention	■ What is our staff turnover rate? ■ What is the employee satisfaction level? ■ What is the impact to customer and/or agent service?	■ Determine cause for unacceptable turnover over rate and take appropriate action ■ Determine reason for poor employee satisfaction and take appropriate action ■ Improve recruitment or training processes	■ Improved employee satisfaction, retention ■ Improved customer and agent service ■ Improved customer and agent satisfaction, retention

Figure B–1 Sales Actionability Framework

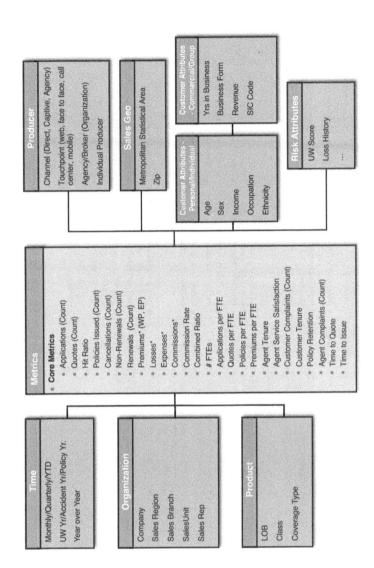

Figure B-2 Sales Dimensionality Framework

Objective	Business Questions/Analysis	Actions	Measureable Results and KPIs
Appropriate Risk Classification, Assessment and Pricing	▪ What risk segment/classification does this risk this class of risks all into? ▪ What are the exposures for this risk/risk class? What is the loss history for this risk/risk class? For this insured/group of insureds? ▪ Does this risk/risk class fall within our current underwriting guidelines? If not, can the exposure/coverage /price be modified to make it acceptable? ▪ What is the proper price for this risk/risk class? ▪ How do we compare to competitors? (price, product, etc.)	▪ Plan strategies on growth and profitability targets ▪ Align products to spread risk and ensure sufficient premium for exposure ▪ Make pricing / terms and conditions adjustments based on individual exposure and loss experience	▪ Meet target segment and product goals (written premium, PIFs and profitability) ▪ Improved risk portfolio profitability (loss ratio, net underwriting profit) ▪ Updated underwriting guidelines
Agent and Customer Satisfaction and Retention	▪ What are our new business trends? (new applications/submissions, quotes, policies issued) ▪ What are our renewals trends? (renewals, cancellations, non-renewals), ▪ What is our customer and agent satisfaction with our products, pricing and service? What are their retention rates?	▪ ID and analyze negative new business trends and take action ▪ ID and analyze negative renewal trends and take action ▪ ID and analyze negative satisfaction trends and take action	▪ Meet new business and renewal goals ▪ Improved customer and agent satisfaction ▪ Improved customer and agent retention
Associate Retention	▪ What is our staff turnover rate? ▪ What is the employee satisfaction level? ▪ What is the impact to customer and/or agent service?	▪ Determine cause for unacceptable turnover over rate and take appropriate action ▪ Determine reason for poor employee satisfaction and take appropriate action ▪ Improve recruitment or training processes	▪ Reduced turnover rate ▪ Improved employee satisfaction ▪ Improved customer and agent service ▪ Improved customer and agent satisfaction ▪ Improved customer and agent retention

Figure B–3 Underwriting Actionability Framework

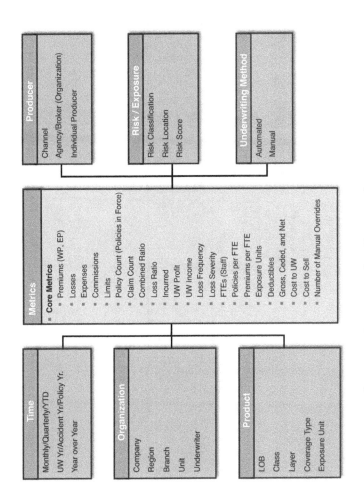

Figure B–4 Underwriting Dimensionality Framework

Objective	Business analysis	Actions	Results (KPIs)
Improve claims productivity	■ Which are our most/least efficient branches? Adjusters? ■ What is our mix of claims events by channel, location, claim associate type? ■ What are our costs for staff vs. outsourced services?	■ Revise business processes ■ Develop claim training based on best practices ■ Outsource claims processes	■ Reduced claim processing costs ■ Increased claim associate retention
Reduce claim indemnity costs	■ What are our indemnity payment trends? ■ How does average incurred by channel compare? ■ What is our average claims recovery for Subro? Salvage?	■ Increased speed of claim settlement ■ Earlier subro, salvage recovery referrals	■ Reduced indemnity costs ■ Increased claims recoveries
Increase customer claim satisfaction	■ What is our claim customer satisfaction? ■ How does it correlate to customer retention?	■ Align customer service preference to channels	■ Increased claim customer satisfaction ■ Increased customer retention

Figure B–5 Claims Actionability Framework

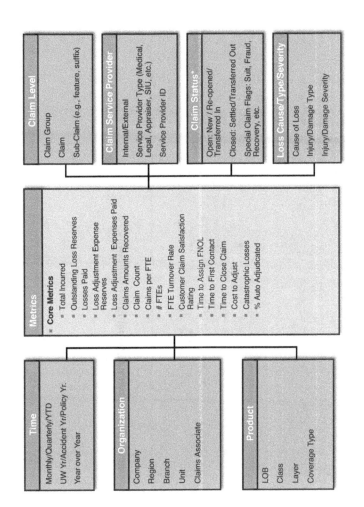

Figure B–6 Claims Dimensionality Framework

Objective	Business analysis	Actions	Results (KPIs)
Improve service productivity and reduce costs	■ Which are our most/least efficient channels? Associates? ■ What is our mix of service events by channel, site, associate type? ■ What are our service costs by channel?	■ Revise business processes ■ Develop service training based on best practices ■ Plan and manage internal / external channels and resources	■ Increased service efficiency/utilization ■ Increased service quality ■ Reduced service costs
Increase customer and producer retention	■ What is the impact of service quality and timeliness on customer and producer retention? ■ What is our customer /producer satisfaction by channel, site, event? ■ What is our customer/producer retention by channel, site, event?	■ Align customer and service channels by profitability ■ Improve customer, producer satisfaction and retention ■ Increase customer revenue (e.g., cross-sell)	■ Increased customer retention, premium ■ Increased number of products by customer ■ Increased producer engagement, revenue
Increase service associate satisfaction and retention	■ What is our service associate satisfaction? Retention ■ How does it correlate to customer and producer retention? Growth?	■ Revise service associate training, incentives ■ Revise channel and resource service plans	■ Increased service associate satisfaction and retention ■ Increased customer and product retention

Figure B-7 Service Actionability Framework

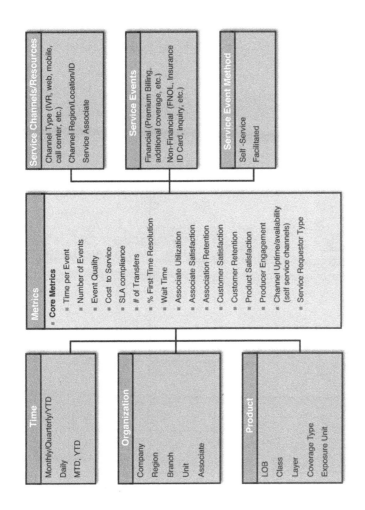

Figure B-8 Service Dimensionality Framework

Figure B-9 Actionability Framework Template

Objective	Business analysis	Actions	Results (KPIs)

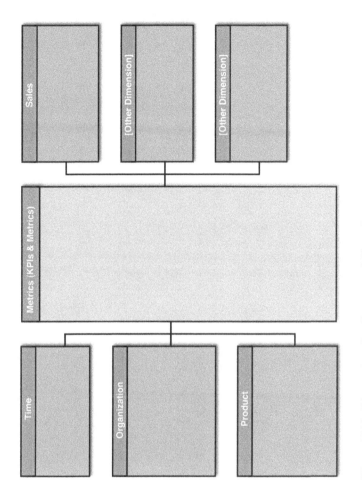

Figure B10 Dimensionality Framework Template

C

Analytics Blogs and Videos

Following is a list of blogs and videos on analytics that the author has written or spoken on, and five business intelligence/Big Data blog posts from the Decision Factor website.

Decision Factor

The Decision Factor (www.the-decisionfactor.com) is a thought-leadership blog on business analytics. The blogs in bold follow in full-text with links to the original blog; additional graphics are included in the original postings. You can also find the other blogs on the Decision Factor site.

- **Two More Big Data V's: Value and Veracity**. January 23, 2014.
- **Your BICC is the Glue That Holds Business and Technology together. December 6, 2013.**
- **Business Intelligence Competency Center: A Key Element of Your BI Program. November 8, 2013.**
- **Business Intelligence Strategy: BICCs Take Center Stage... Again! July 31, 2013.**
- Data to Decision: Big Insights vs. Big Data. May 7, 2013.
- **Designing the Intelligence Enterprise. March 4, 2013**.
- **Data Discovery: A Key Tool for Big Data Insights. August 6, 2012.**
- Insuring ROI on Big Data. April 24, 2012.

BI and Your Success, a YouTube Playlist

BI and Your Success is a five-part thought-leadership video series available on YouTube. (http://www.youtube.com/playlist?list=PLufF7pZxIC BjHeO4WY-kJ_KNpEuBgfH4f)

- "Developing a Business Intelligence Strategy." Deepa Sankar.

- "Developing a Business Intelligence Competency Center." Pat Saporito.

- "Progressing Along the Business Intelligence Maturity Curve." Colin Dover.

- "Building a Business Case for Business Intelligence Strategy." Imran Siddiqi.

- "Forging an Information Culture: BI and Your Success." Laura Jamieson.

C1: Designing the Intelligent Enterprise

Organizations are jumping on the big data bandwagon—but all too often, the driver is performance and the platform. Even though both are important, starting there is like putting the cart before the horse. It can leave you scurrying to find business initiatives to justify your platform investment and ongoing funding.

The value in Big Data is what your business can do with it—you can distinguish yourself from the rest of the pack by becoming an intelligent enterprise through transformation and innovation. To do this, you need to anticipate market trends and, ideally, create them. The new analytics world is not your father's business intelligence world that consisted of reporting historical data. No, the new analytics world is forward looking and real-time: it involves social media, predictive modeling, and telematics.

Innovation requires a business vision enabled by technology. It also takes the use of transforming skills to create your own Art of the Possible. Creating this vision means defining truly compelling use cases that match your core capabilities to timely market opportunities.

One way to create this vision is with "Design Thinking," an approach that is empathetic and places you in your customer's shoes. This involves brainstorming market and product opportunities by assuming a customer persona. In this way, you can identify with customer pains and brainstorm new approaches to products, solutions, and actions to solve those pains.

After going through this process, you'll be ready to prioritize potential solutions, establish market potential and value, and evaluate your current abilities and gaps. From there, you can determine which existing abilities will suffice, which ones need enhancement, and which ones need to be developed.

As you build your solutions and applications, you can also start to drive true self-service analytics by engaging employees in data exploration and predictive thinking, as well, for ongoing continuous improvement.

The greatest benefit of this approach is that you begin to transform everyone's mindset to an innovative one that is truly customer-driven.

Link: http://www.the-decisionfactor.com/business-analytics-strategy/designing-the-intelligent-enterprise/#sthash.37xwQINV.dpuf

Original posting: The Decision Factor, Feb. 21, 2013 www.the-decision-factor.com

C2: Data Discovery: A Key Tool for Big Data Insights

As data volumes and varieties grow, more organizations are looking for ways to get value out of their Big Data. Data discovery, an advanced analytic capability, enables business analysts to discover insights in their data without depending on IT to create subsets/business views or merge/cleanse the data. Using new data discovery and visualization tools, analysts can now conduct discovery themselves, find insights, and share them with other users, speeding up "insight to action" for competitive advantage. After all it's the business users who best understand their own data and can readily see threats and opportunities through that data.

As you review these new tools for use in your own organization, keep in mind the key abilities and caveats and common business applications for self-service business intelligence (BI) listed here.

- Agility and high performance for faster data exploration and combining large data sets

- Real-time analysis for operational business intelligence to find insights and take immediate action on them

- Flexibility to combine multiple data sources easily—without IT's help

- Easy to use and learn

- Visual appeal and a large choice of graphic display options to communicate insights effectively

- Dashboards that are easy for users to create

- Access via smartphones, tablets, and other mobile devices

- Collaboration so it's easy to share and take action on insights

- Built-in data manipulation (for example, hierarchy creation) without scripting or programming

Although all these end-user features should be included in your selection criteria, consideration should also be given to a tool's capability to integrate into your broader business intelligence suite for ad-hoc reporting, formatted reporting, predictive analysis, and other BI actions—all of which complement self-service capabilities in data discovery tools. Organizations should also beware of selecting multiple self-service tools across end-user area, which can create more islands of data, different user interfaces, and interoperability issues.

The following areas are common business applications for data discovery tools:

- **Increasing revenue:** Two common, cross-industry marketing applications are customer and distribution analysis. Both are used to identify characteristics for market and channel segmentation in relation to marketing campaigns. Similarly in sales, product revenue and margin analysis enable you to see into volume, profitability, and profitability drivers, so you can sell more profitable products and less unprofitable ones and determine the necessary changes to make products more profitable.

- **Reducing risk:** Another common application across many industries is fraud detection. Whether for claims fraud (insurance), inventory "leakage" (retail), or credit card fraud (banking), data discovery can help identify outliers that may indicate fraud and clusters of fraud characteristics before you run your data mining.

- **Decreasing expenses:** Data discovery also helps optimize business process efficiency and workforce productivity through best- and worst-performance analysis and benchmarking. In fact, a placebo effect is often realized just from sharing of best and worst performance benchmarks, resulting in a performance lift. You can make substantial improvements when you apply the actions/findings in business process reengineering, training, or incentive/talent-management and workforce-scheduling applications.

Regardless of the tool you choose, the most important thing is to start. Use it against your data, analyze, share/collaborate on your findings, take action, and measure the results. This closed-loop process allows you to leverage the value in your data assets and move the needle to improve your market performance.

Bottom line: Most organizations have well-conquered descriptive business intelligence (looking backward at what happened). The value in Big Data lies in prescriptive business intelligence and using self-service BI tools such as data discovery to determine what will happen and how to capitalize on it.

Link: http://www.the-decisionfactor.com/business-intelligence/data-discovery-a-key-tool-for-big-data-insights/#sthash.fnesr7AX.dpuf

Original posting: The Decision Factor, July 31, 2012 www.the-decision-factor.com

C3: Business Intelligence Strategy: BICCs Take Center Stage...Again!

(Part 1 of 3 in a series on BI Competency Centers)

As data grows in size and complexity and organizations struggle to meet the ever-increasing demand for analytics, BI Competency Centers (BICCs) are in the spotlight once more. Ironically, despite the projected 80% annual growth in data and the projection of 50% of enterprise employees use of analytics by 2014 (and 75% by 2020), most organizations today have only a 10% BI adoption rate. Including an effective BI Competency Center as part of your overall BI Strategy is a critical element in increasing BI adoption, enabling BI self-service, and ensuring that your organization has the right analytic capabilities to deliver analytic business value.

A BICC, also called a BI Center of Excellence, is part of a BI Strategy Framework. It incorporates governance, program management, BI strategy roadmap and milestones, education and training, and support. A BICC is a cross-functional team with specific tasks, roles, responsibilities, and processes for supporting and promoting the effective use of BI across organizations (Gartner 2001). BICCs are largely engaged in the organization and implementation areas of a BI strategy.

BICCs are also part of an overall BI Maturity Model but have their own maturity development. They evolve from the following:

1. No BICC, to

2. An IT/technology driven BICC (usually focused on architecture and products), to

3. A business-driven BICC (business needs driven), and ultimately, to

4. A mature BICC

The BICC development process involves continuous improvement and should be a key element reviewed at least annually as part of your overall BI strategy review and update. Business needs change and new capabilities are needed to adapt to business and enabling technology advances.

You can see a BICC's evolution in the BI governance area of the maturity model.

BICCs can take a number of organizational forms or models depending on your organization. The different types of models and benefits of a BICC are discussed in the author's blog.

Link: http://www.the-decisionfactor.com/business-intelligence/ business-intelligence-strategy-bi-competency-centers-take-center-stage-again/#sthash.0GjcQX2v.dpuf

Original Posting: The Decision Factor, July 23, 2013 www.the-decision-factor.com

C4: Business Intelligence Strategy: BICC, A Key Element of Your BI Program.

(Part 2 of 3 in a series on BI Competency Centers)

In my last blog, I discussed the importance of a Business Intelligence Competency Center for any organization working on taking its BI program to the highest level of competency. In this edition, I'll focus on different types of BICC organizational models.

BICCs can take a number of organizational forms or models—the most common are the BICC as part of IT, a virtual BICC, BICC as part of operations, or a distributed BICC. BICCs often start out in a distributed or virtual form. Each model has its own pros and cons, and your organization is likely to change as it matures. The best model fit for your organization depends on your culture, but one or more models will work in your environment.

BICCs create many improvements in business intelligence (BI) and analytics. The top three benefits are

- Better collaboration between business and IT, ensuring a business driven BI/analytics strategy

- Increased use/adoption of BI and analytic investments through best practices, evangelization, and "sand boxes"

- Improved data quality and data management, enabling more time for analysis versus preparation and validation

These three areas should ultimately result in increased revenue, decreased expenses, and improved operational efficiency.

BICCs face a number of challenges, but two key related ones are visibility and funding. Having a BICC champion at the senior management level is a must. But even with an executive champion, the BICC's value may not be fully recognized. Define measureable KPIs and communicate them through a BICC dashboard or scorecard for awareness.

Most frequently used metrics are in delivered return areas, such as pipeline, cost, usage, and quality and operational performance areas such as uptime, load time, outage, and education. Post the dashboard on a BICC wiki or community, post your charter, tout BI success stories, post upcoming educational courses/webcasts, and add links to analytic sandboxes. BICCs that keep awareness of their capabilities and value front and center struggle far less with funding than those that aren't visible.

If you don't have a BICC, then you need the basics of building an organization.

- Find an executive champion.

- Define your charter/mission.

- Decide on your form, define roles, and fill with the right candidates.

- Layout a roadmap for the BICC, initial versus near future state.

- Launch the BICC, focusing on defining your strategy and documenting/amassing current BI-related standards and processes.

If you already have a BICC, evaluate what you need to do to take it to the next level. Conduct a BICC assessment as part of an annual BI strategy review.

- Review your current and projected 18-month business intelligence capabilities with the business areas. Identify pains/issues and rank them based on anticipated business value.

- Review your current BICC state by addressing governance, program management, education, support, and so on. Assess your current level—both the existence and completeness of these capabilities. Rank areas for improvement based on anticipated business value.

- Review gaps in your current BI strategy and BICC. Identify areas of improvement and rank them.

- Create a BI strategy and BICC roadmap to close the gaps.

For more on BICCs, read my first blog in the series, "Business Intelligence Strategy: BI Competency Centers Take Center Stage... Again!," and be watching for the next blog soon.

Link: http://www.the-decisionfactor.com/business-intelligence/bi-strategy-bicc-a-key-element-of-your-bi-program/#sthash.FGwxMuWI.dpuf

Original Posting: The Decision Factor, Nov. 5, 2013 www.the-decision-factor.com

C5: Your BICC Is the Glue That Holds Business and Technology Together: Skill, Roles, and Guerilla Tactics for Promotion

(Part 3 of 3 in a Series on BI Competency Centers)

As I described in my first blog in this series, BICCs are critical to the success of an organization's analytics. They are chartered to align business-driven objectives with information, applications, processes, training, policies, and technology regardless of the size of an organization. Their capabilities span human capital, knowledge processes, culture, and infrastructure. Yet many organizations struggle with where to start or how to evolve their BICCs.

I also reviewed BICC organizational models in an earlier blog. In this one, I'll discuss the skill sets, key roles, and responsibilities required for a successful BICC. I'll also review some low risk, high impact "guerilla" tactics to get your BICC off the ground and to sustain its ongoing visibility.

Skills needed by effective BICCs fall into three key broad areas: business, IT, and analytics. The capabilities needed within each of these areas are

- **Business skills:** Linking to business strategy, defining priorities, leading organization and process change, and controlling funding. These often sit in the business, but IT needs to develop as well.

- **IT skills:** Defining vision, maintaining programs, establishing standards, creating the technology roadmap, providing methodology leadership, maintaining an adaptable infrastructure, and improving data quality. These are traditionally technical skills, but business users need an awareness of these skills, especially standards and roadmap, which play a key role in data quality.

- **Analytics skills:** Developing user skills, defining business rules, identifying and extracting data, creating business views of data, discovering and exploring data, and enabling advanced analytical skills like statistical and text mining. Analytic skills are needed across the organization both in business and IT areas.

There are a myriad of roles required by BICCs. But bear in mind, they don't all need to reside within the BICC. Some can be virtual roles that actually reside in the business, such as business analysts and data stewards. I'm purposely omitting development roles (programmers, data modelers, architects) that reside in an IT BI development team or in distributed business BI development areas. I'm also leaving out the role of business analyst, which is critical to an ongoing program and may reside in the business, IT, or BICC. The key roles that do need to exist within a BICC include

- **BICC leader:** Manages overall BICC program and BICC as well as vendor relationships, licensing, internal user groups, and metadata. Leads analytic adoption. Ensures business alignment. Sets and monitors BICC key performance indicators. Secures funding. Aligns with executive and BI steering committee.

- **Chief data steward:** Manages overall data governance and related initiatives, for example, metadata management. Works with the data architect/data manager to develop the data architecture. Identifies issues and recommends actions to address data quality and integrity. Chairs data governance committee and is a member of BI steering committee.

- **Knowledge management leader:** Manages the overall KM practices, policies, and procedures to maximize adoption of BICC capabilities. Includes BI standards, templates, and so on. Identifies new training programs needed as well as "currentness" of existing training programs.

- **BICC support leader:** Manages overall BICC support and ensures that user support issues are addressed.

- **BICC technical leader:** Manages technical environment for analytics. Ensures correct technical setup of BI solutions and advises on any connectivity, security, or other technical capabilities required. Secondary support for BICC service desk. Often includes managing analytic application selection and license administration.

- **BICC communication leader:** Communicates activities, plans, and progress on current project. Creates intranet, community, or other vehicle to communicate and build awareness of BI program progress and success.

It's important to pick projects that can be successful and to develop user evangelists that can help you sell successful projects. This will help you gain credibility and ensure ongoing funding for the BICC. Here are some tips, or "Guerilla Tactics" for getting your BICC off the ground:

- **Celebrate Success**
  - Pick a first initiative and make it a business success.
  - Stand up the BICC roles to support the initiative.
  - Identify evangelists from the initiative and have them sell the success.

- **Sell the Sizzle**
  - Use dashboards, scorecards, maps, and other visual applications/tools.
  - Analytics is "white hot," so sell it.

- **Go Beyond Reporting**
  - Stress self-service capabilities and analysis versus reporting.
  - Make it easy to use—use the right tool and make sure end users are trained.
  - Help users internalize BI as part of their success—drive culture change.

- **Communicate**
  - Create a BICC community and engage users to provide feedback.
  - Make it interactive and fun—develop an internal or external contest they can participate in, for example. This is also a form of learning as well as recognition.
  - Highlight successes, best practices, and new capabilities on the community.

Understanding the key roles and responsibilities needed for BICCs is critical to the success of your BICC and your overall BI strategy. It's also important to understand the skills needed for these roles and to either look for them during your hiring process, or include them as part of professional development for existing business and technical staff.

Link: http://www.the-decisionfactor.com/business-intelligence/ your-bicc-is-the-glue-that-holds-business-and-technology-to- gether-skills-roles-and-guerilla-tactics-for-promotion/#sthash. Or1HYOTn.dpuf

Original Posting: The Decision Factor, Dec. 3, 2013
www.the-decisionfactor.com

Index

S

T

U

UBI (usage-based insurance), 123
UM (utilization management), 134
underwriting, 122-123
  business needs
    Analytics Actionability Framework, 26-27
    Dimensional Analysis, 30-32
    discovery interviews, 25
    use cases, 28-30
  prioritization, 32
underwriting actionability framework, 154
underwriting analytics, 6
underwriting dimensionality framework, 4, 155
UnitedHealth Group's "Numbers" Advertising Campaign, 109
UnitedHealth Group, network management, 135
unstructured data analytics tools, text mining, 84-85
usability of analytics, 7
usage-based insurance (UBI), 123
use cases
  business needs, underwriting, 28-30
  claims, 126-127
  disease and wellness management, 133-134
  ERM (enterprise risk management), 131-133
  finance, 129-130
  health insurance analytics, 133
  life insurance analytics, 135-136
  marketing, 116-117
  policy/contract administration and service, 125
  product management, 115

property and casualty value chain, 114-115
provider and network management, 134-135
sales and distribution management, 120-121
underwriting, 122-123
user categories, structured data tool types and, 83-84
user support, BICCs (BI Competency Centers), 96
users of analytics, 7
utilization management (UM), 134

V

value
  BI Strategy Framework, 14
  BICCs (BI Competency Centers), 92-93
  business discovery, 146-147
value chains, 105
Value Discovery, 49-50
value life cycle, 51
value management, 57
Value Optimization, 50-51
Value Realization, 50
value-based approach, BI performance opportunities and benchmarks for IT, 56-57
Value-Based Management, 49-51
  Value Discovery, 49-50
  value life cycle, 51
  Value Optimization, 50-51
  Value Realization, 50
Variety, 45
Velocity, 45
virtual BICC, 97
visualization tools, 9
Volume, 45

X-Y

XBRL (extended business reporting
 language), 65, 130

Z

Zurich North American, 117